SHAPING A CITY

BELFAST IN THE LATE TWENTIETH CENTURY

FREDERICK W. BOAL

WITH THE ASSISTANCE OF
JAHNET GARDINER
GAIL SHIELDS
DAVID SPENCE

THE INSTITUTE OF IRISH STUDIES
THE QUEEN'S UNIVERSITY OF BELFAST

COVER ILLUSTRATION, JAMES WILLIAMSON'S MAP OF BELFAST 1791. REPRODUCED WITH
KIND PERMISSION OF THE GOVERNORS OF THE LINENHALL LIBRARY

02-392

First published 1995
by the Institute of Irish Studies
The Queen's University of Belfast
University Road, Belfast

for
The Northern Ireland Housing Executive

ISBN 0 85389 605 4

Printed by Graham & Heslip Ltd

Designed by Gail Shields

PREFACE

Shaping a City attempts to plot the course of Belfast over the past three turbulent decades. It is as if we have been watching helmsmen and helmswomen struggling to establish a route for the city to follow and then, with great difficulty, trying to keep it on course set. Belfast has been buffeted by strong winds that have frequently changed direction - some local in origin, others national and, indeed, international. The storms that have struck have been economic, ethno-national and demographic. In consequence there have been radical changes to many aspects of the city; other things, however, have barely changed at all.

In some ways Belfast's story is unique; in others it is just a specific manifestation in one locale of processes to be found at work in many cities across the globe. In the latter instance Belfast provides a fascinating and instructive story in its own right offering useful lessons of wide applicability.

Shaping a City is one person's attempt to tell this story. Others might wish to tell the story differently. Here I use the written word, graphs, maps and photographs to tell the tale. The illustrations are as much a tool in the story-telling as are the words. They should be seen as such.

At the end of the volume a substantial Bibliography is provided, together with an Appendix containing thirteen tables. The Bibliography and the Appendix are offered for the use of those readers who may wish to follow up some of the topics here examined .

Publication of **Shaping a City** has been timed for the September 1995 Congress of the International Federation for Housing and Planning. The original stimulus for the preparation of this volume was provided by Victor Blease, Chief Executive of the Northern Ireland Housing Executive. The production stages have been enthusiastically supported by Brian Henderson, Head of Information and Secretariat at the Housing Executive. Central to the whole effort have been the contributions of three people -

Jahnet Gardiner, who gathered together much of the material,
Gail Shields who has applied her creative skills to the project
through her use of the Housing Executive's Desk-Top Publishing facility,
and David Spence who has brought his technical and artistic talents to bear
on matters photographic.
All three have contributed in ways well beyond the call of duty.
It has been a real pleasure to work with them.

Many other people have contributed data, photographs, maps, comment and correction. Amongst these should be mentioned Gill Alexander, Michael Henderson, Trevor McCartney, John McPeake and Maura Pringle.

The last line has to be the usual disclaimer. I alone am responsible for the structure and contents of the book, including any matters of interpretation.

Fred Boal
Department of Geography,
School of Geosciences,
The Queen's University of Belfast.
September 1995

Contents

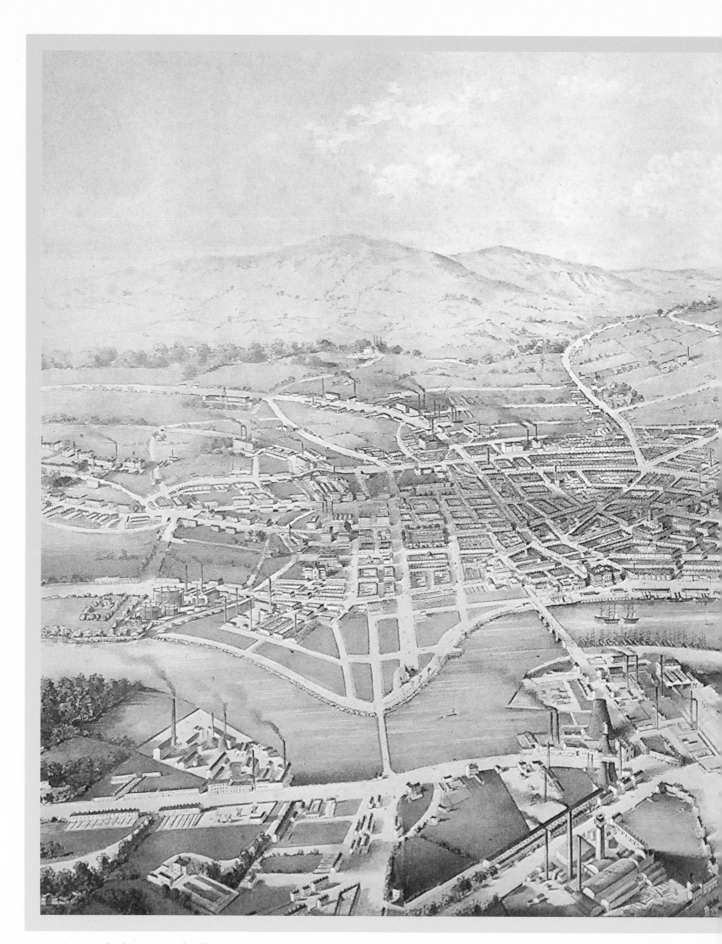

J.H Connop's bird's eye view of Belfast 1863

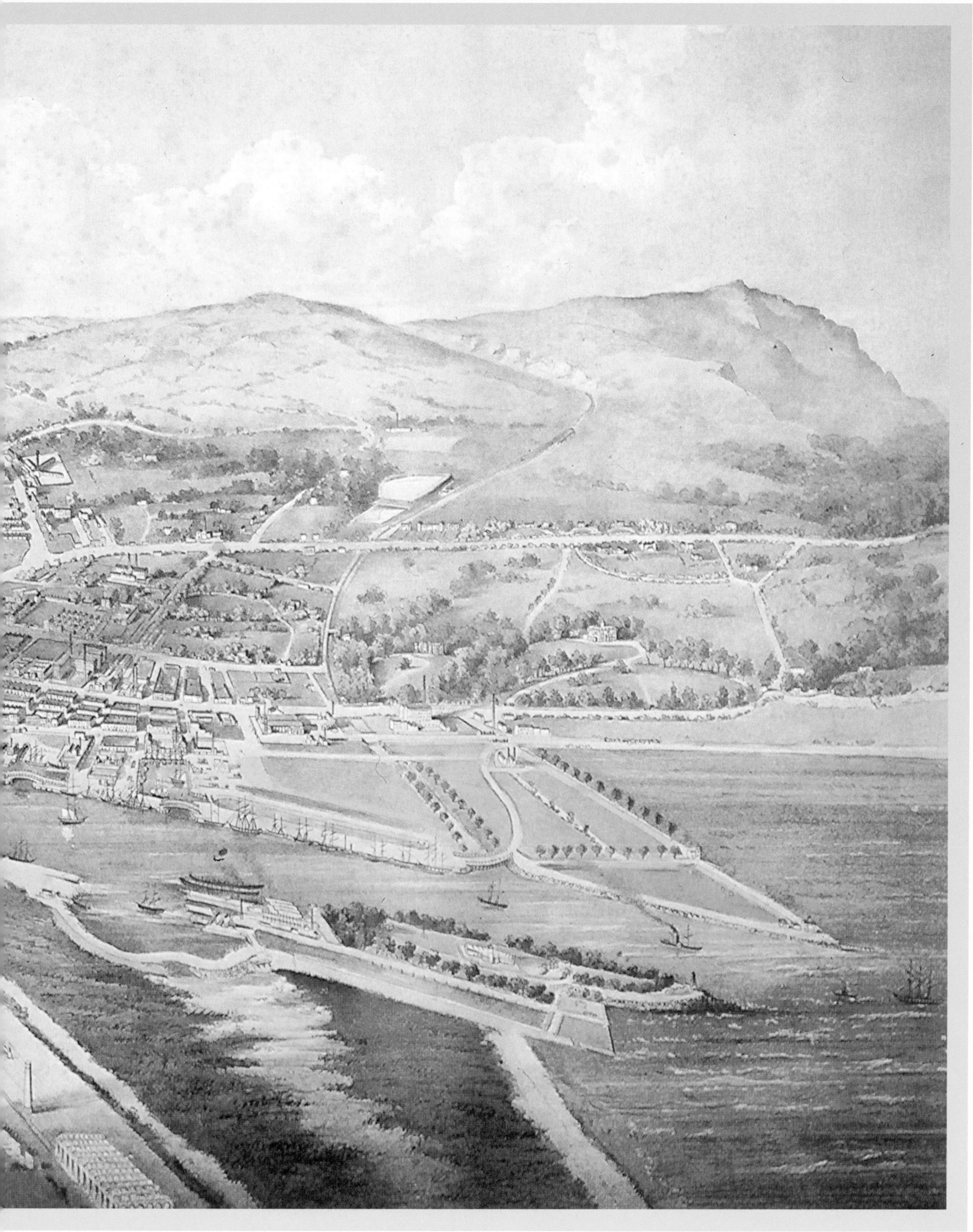

Linenhall Library

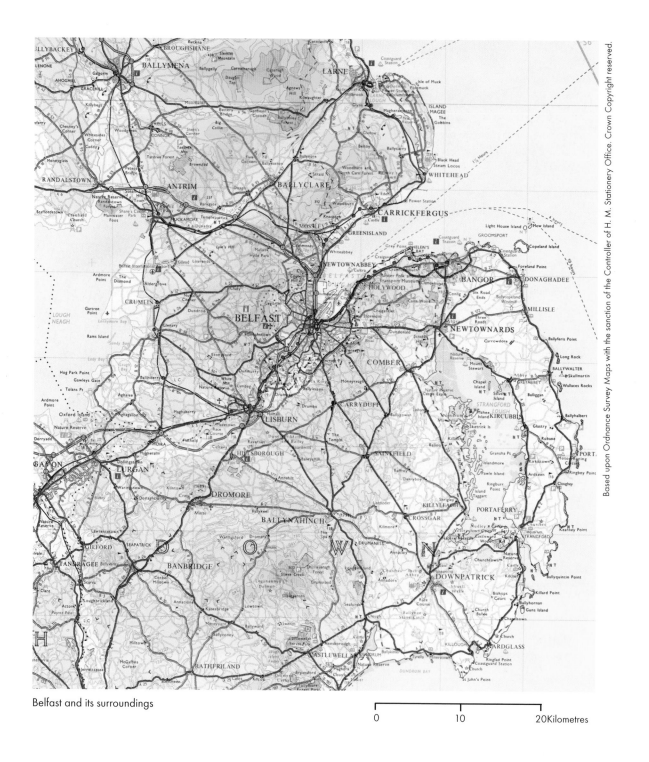

Belfast and its surroundings

Based upon Ordnance Survey Maps with the sanction of the Controller of H. M. Stationery Office. Crown Copyright reserved.

Chapter 1 - Where and When
From the beginnings to the 1960s
A little history to start with

Site and situation

Belfast clings to the sea and is hugged by the land. The nucleus of the city was set at a point where the River Lagan completed its wandering lower course by slowly discharging into Belfast Lough. The Lough itself is an intrusion of the Irish Sea into the north east of Ireland. It has long provided a two-way channel of communication between Belfast and the outside world. Over the past two hundred years the Lough has suffered a steady retreat at the hands of a city vigorously claiming the tidal mud-flats and converting them into urban land ~ land albeit with strong maritime connections (shipbuilding, marine engineering, port facilities).

Constraining the Lough and, in many places, containing the growth of the city are the hills to the north-west and south-east. In the former direction lies the southern edge of the Antrim plateau, an edge noted for its steep, and in one place, precipitous slopes. In the latter direction lies the more subdued hills of north Down ~ providing a hint of green rurality above the city, contrasting with the somewhat foreboding and more massive presence of the Antrim slopes, some 8 kilometres (5 miles) away across the Lagan Valley.

The Lagan Valley itself, squeezed by the hills and, in its lowest section, flooded by Belfast Lough, provides a corridor from the sea to the central lowland heart of Northern Ireland. Prehistoric route-ways, an eighteenth century canal, roadways, a railway line and now a motorway all have used the valley floor. As the city has grown, it has filled the valley, risen up the slopes of the containing hills, expanded up the Lagan Valley, stretched along both shores of Belfast Lough and spilled out of the valley itself to the north, the east and the south east.

History

Pre-historically, and through much of the historic period, the site of Belfast was a low-lying, swampy place. It gained whatever significance it had from the fact that the River Lagan could be forded nearby. Settlement avoided the lowland, preferring the nearby hill slopes.

The first recorded construction at what was to be Belfast was a castle built by the Anglo-Normans in the 1170s as they sought to form a network of fortified places the better to secure control of the coastal margins of eastern Ireland.

The seventeenth century plantation of Ulster, when England sought to subdue the northern part of Ireland, really marks the emergence of Belfast as a significant settlement. The castle was rebuilt, Protestant settlers were attracted and an earth rampart was constructed to protect the settlement against the Irish.

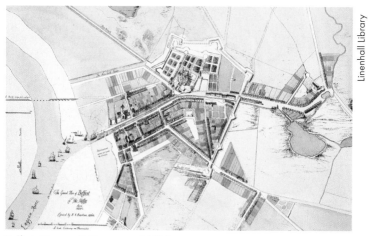

Belfast: Thomas Phillips map of 1685

Belfast grew slowly through the eighteenth century. A market in brown linen opened, while the more refined white linen emerged later in the century, marked by the opening of the White Linen Hall (on the site of the present City Hall) in 1785.

Linenhall Library

White Linen Hall

Initially linen production was a rural activity, Belfast serving as one of the market centres. At the end of the century, however, cotton manufacture began in the city, based on water power. This laid a foundation for the rapid nineteenth century expansion of textile manufacture, an activity that became completely dominated by linen. Shipbuilding and engineering also began to emerge as significant activities, the latter, at least in part, linked to textiles.

Ulster Museum

Nineteenth century linen weaving

The booming industrialization of the first half of the nineteenth century drew large numbers of migrants from the rural areas of the northern part of Ireland. This not only contributed to rapid population growth; it also introduced a significant Catholic component to what had previously been an overwhelmingly Protestant town. From a mere five percent in the mid eighteenth century, the Catholic population grew slowly to ten percent by 1800, followed by a rapid increase, both in absolute numbers and in proportion, so that by the 1830s Catholics comprised about one-third of a population of some 50,000. Catholic-Protestant friction grew with this

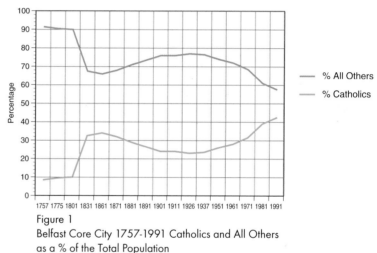

Figure 1
Belfast Core City 1757-1991 Catholics and All Others as a % of the Total Population

expansion. As Bill Maguire points out, in his history of Belfast, an influx of Irish Catholic labour was a common feature of nineteenth century industrialization not only in Belfast but also in cities in Britain such as Glasgow, Liverpool and Manchester. All had their inter-ethnic tensions, but in the case of Belfast these *"were to prove in everyway sharper, more persistent and more divisive than anywhere else."* Evocatively, Maguire describes this movement *"as Catholic counter-colonization,"* importing with it intense feelings of territoriality, common enough at the time for both Protestants and Catholics in rural areas to the west.

The second half of the nineteenth century saw Belfast firmly established as a major industrial centre ~ both as Linenopolis and as home to the largest shipyard and the largest rope-works in the world. In the forty years from 1861, Belfast's population grew from 121,000 to 350,000, the latter number making the city larger than Dublin at the time. The numbers of Catholics continued to increase, though their proportion of the population declined, the former being more significant in sectarian calculations.

The end of the nineteenth century saw a huge boom in house construction. These were built to standards higher than had prevailed earlier elsewhere ~ thus avoiding most of the back-to-backs of industrial Britain.

By 1911 Belfast's population had reached 386,000. The first decade of the twentieth century saw a rather uneven industrial expansion, but the completion of the new City Hall in 1906 was a powerful statement and symbol of civic confidence. However, conflict over Irish Home Rule cast a long shadow on the city, relieved briefly by the economic boom of World War I. While the economy continued to thrive until the late 1920s, communal strife greatly intensified as Belfast became capital city of a newly formed province of the United Kingdom ~ Northern Ireland.

City Hall - completed in 1906

As the twenties became the thirties, so a world-wide economic slump seriously undermined Belfast's core industries ~ heavily dependent as they were on export markets. A growing shortage of jobs sharpened ethnic sectarian rivalry, with serious disturbances in the city causing major population movement and a sharpening of residential segregation between Catholics and Protestants. There was a period of two years in the 1930s when Harland and Wolff launched no ships, while the other Belfast shipyard (Workman Clark and Company) closed down completely in 1935. The only major industrial bright spot was the arrival of the aircraft manufacturers Shorts, who by 1939 were employing 6,000 workers.

World War II, as with the 1914-18 conflict, gave a new boost to Belfast industry ~ particularly aircraft, shipbuilding and engineering. A heavy price was paid for this however, as German bombers attacked the city on several occasions in an attempt (in the short term successful) to disrupt production. In addition to damage and destruction to industrial and commercial premises, almost 57,000 houses were destroyed or damaged and over a thousand people killed. Mass evacuations of citizens, together with bomb damage, revealed, to many for the first time, the appalling housing conditions that existed in inner Belfast. This revelation, in turn, led to calls for a vigorous housing campaign, something quite new for a city that had only constructed two and a half thousand public sector dwellings between 1918 and 1939.

Ulster Museum

Titanic and Olympic under construction at Harland and Wolff 1910

Harland and Wolff Shipyard: Cranes over the building dock

High levels of wartime employment continued for some years thereafter, though the decline in ship-building and linen manufacture that had commenced in the 1930s, re-emerged. This was particularly true for linen. Shipbuilding fared much better for a time as British yards strove to replace tonnage lost during the war. Through the 1960s linen continued to decline, while Harland and Wolff laid plans to convert their shipyard to the new techniques of the building dock, in the process abandoning slipway build and launch. In consequence of this, the great industrial landmarks of twentieth century Belfast became the two huge Goliath cranes, yellow and rectangular dominants in the city's skyline.

CHAPTER II - POPULATION SINCE THE 1960s
The number of people in the city and their distribution provide key indicators of change

Belfast City Council, Parks and Amenities Section

Inner Belfast: late nineteenth and early twentieth century terrace housing east of the Lagan (note the redevelopment of the 1970s and 1980s)

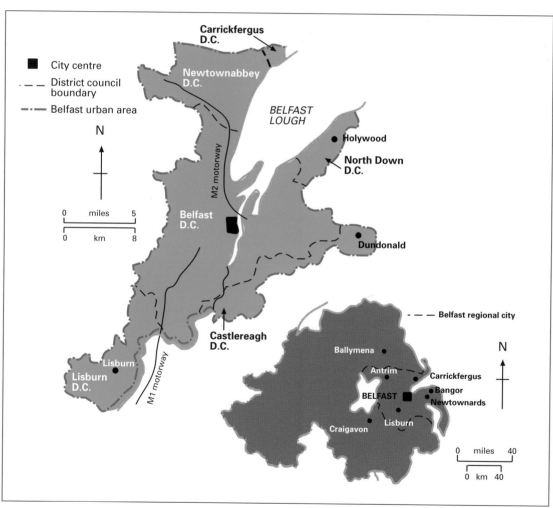

Figure 2
Belfast Urban Area and Regional City 1995

Counting People

If we want to monitor what is happening to a city we can do no better than examine various aspects of its population. For present purposes we will look at population size and at the number of units into which the population is organized (households). We will then go on to explore a particularly important dimension of the city's population ~ its division along ethnic/religious lines. Finally we will briefly look at how the population is composed in terms of age.

Before looking at population numbers, however, we need to decide on what we mean by Belfast. In the nineteenth century Belfast was basically a continuously built-up area that was almost entirely contained within the politically defined city. The twentieth century, however, has seen the built-up area expand well beyond the political limits. Moreover, an even more extensive area needs to be noted, much of which is not a continuously built-up extension of the older city. Rather it is a discontinuously urbanized region that is tied to the traditional city by being within the heavily travelled commuter zone.

Thus we recognize three basic rings of urbanization ~ the Core City of Belfast (defined by the city's political boundary), the continuously built up area beyond (together with the core city this makes up the Belfast Urban Area (BUA)) and the commuter settlements beyond that again (together with the Belfast Urban Area this makes up the Regional City) (Figure 2). When we come to look at what has happened over the past two decades or so it will be useful to define a further zone ~ the Inner Core City, which corresponds roughly with what was (until redevelopment) the oldest part of the urban area.

What we recognize as the Core City had its greatest growth towards the end of the nineteenth century and in the first decade of the twentieth (Figure 3). The most dramatic decade of all was between 1891 and 1901 when the population grew by 93,000 (an annual average increase of 9,300 persons). Growth began to slow during the early part of the twentieth century, and almost ceased as mid-century

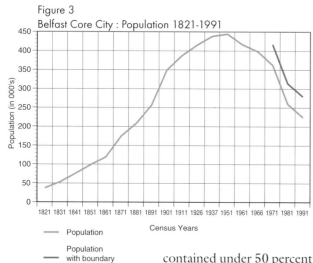

Figure 3
Belfast Core City : Population 1821-1991

approached. From then on the Core Citypopulation went into decline, a decline at its sharpest between 1971 and 1981 when there was a net loss of some 100,000 persons (a decline on average of 10,200 people per year).

As the Core City's growth began to slow, with subsequent movement into a situation of population loss, urban development spread increasingly beyond the limits of the politically bounded city. In 1926, 90 percent of the Belfast Urban Area's population resided in theCore City; little change occurred in the 1930s and 1940s. Thereafter the Core City proportion dropped to 83 percent by 1951, 74 percent by 1961, and 60 percent by 1971. By the beginning of the 1990s the Core City contained under 50 percent of the BUA population, despite a boundary extension in the early 1970s. The greatest burst of sub-urbanization into the BUA fringe is recorded between the censuses of 1951 and 1971. Thereafter suburban population growth sharply declined as urban spread came up against a combination of topographic barriers and planning limitations.

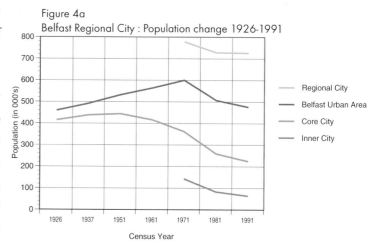

Figure 4a
Belfast Regional City : Population change 1926-1991

We can examine the dynamics of Belfast's population by looking at Figure 4a. The Core City population begins to decline from 1951 onwards, a process that accelerates through the 1960s, almost literally plunging down in the 1970s. The population of the urban area (BUA), on the other hand, maintains a steady climb from the 1920s until 1971 when it reached almost 600,000. Thereafter a radical turn-round takes place, with a rapid fall in the 1970s, slowing through the 1980s. The BUA population decline over these two decades is due entirely to Core City population loss ~ during the same period the suburban fringe, in fact, shows a small growth. (Figure 4b)

During the 1971-1991 period, the Regional City as a whole declined in population by some seven percent, almost all of it during the 1970s. This pattern is composed of two countervailing tendencies ~ on the one hand the dramatic Core City decline, and, on the other, an equally dramatic growth in the outer reaches of the Regional City. Thus while the Core City population decreased by 33 percent between 1971 and 1991, the Outer Regional City grew by 39 percent. The 1991 distribution of population in the component parts of the Regional City is shown in Figure 5.

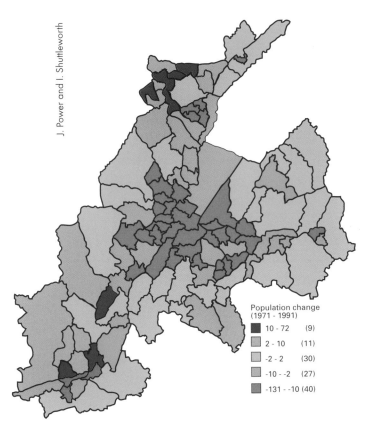

J. Power and I. Shuttleworth

Population change
(1971 - 1991)

■	10 - 72	(9)
▨	2 - 10	(11)
▨	-2 - 2	(30)
▨	-10 - -2	(27)
■	-131 - -10	(40)

Figure 4b
Belfast Urban Area: population change 1971-1991
(change in number of persons per hectare)

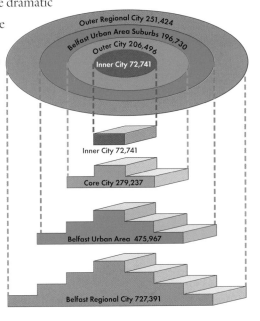

Outer Regional City 251,424
Belfast Urban Area Suburbs 196,730
Outer City 206,496
Inner City 72,741

Inner City 72,741

Core City 279,237

Belfast Urban Area 475,967

Belfast Regional City 727,391

Figure 5
Belfast Regional City: Population in component parts 1991

Households

While the number of people in the Regional City and its constituent parts provides an important indicator of what has been happening to Belfast, the number of households is also significant, particularly when it comes to questions of housing supply and demand.

There is a crucial difference in the pattern of change in numbers of households compared with numbers of people. For instance, between 1971 and 1991 the Regional City population declined by seven percent, but households increased by fifteen percent. At the same time average household size has declined ~ from 3.3 persons per household in 1971 to 2.82 in 1991. The biggest change is in single person households, with a rise of almost 120 percent in the twenty year period. Elderly households have also shown significant gain ~ up by 35 percent.

Figure 6
Belfast Regional City 1971-1991: Changes in population and in numbers of households

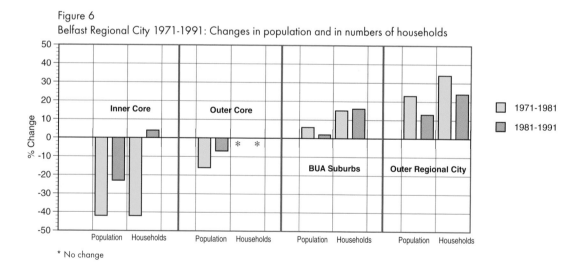

* No change

Figure 6 indicates the change in population and households for the four component segments of the Regional City. The Urban Area suburbs show population and household gain in both the 1971-81 and 1981-91 decades but households have increased proportionately to a much greater extent than population (households up by 37 percent between 1971 and 1991, population up by 8 percent). The Outer Regional City population increased by 39 percent over the twenty years 1971-1991, but household increase far outstripped this, gaining 66 percent in the same two decades.

Terrace Housing 1973 (Inner City) -
Lower Falls

The Core City shows a similar relationship between population and household change, but the overall pattern here is characterized by decline. Over the twenty year period the Inner Core City lost 55 percent of its population but only 39 percent of its households; the Outer Core City suffered a 22 percent population reduction, while the number of households remained constant. Finally, Inner Core City experience points up a further significant feature. In the 1971-1981 decade population and household losses were at almost the same rate (a loss of 42 percent compared to a loss of 41 percent). In the 1981-91 decade, however, while population decline continued, albeit at a slower rate, there was an actual *increase* in the number of households (up by four percent). From this it would appear that the 1971-1981 decade saw a general uprooting of existing households; the 1981-1991 decade saw a more selective process of change, with a continued thinning of population juxtaposed to a growing number of single person and single parent family households. Thus emerges an apparently contradictory phenomenon ~ declining population on the one hand and increasing demand for dwelling units on the other. Of course the *types* of dwellings demanded in the new situation are likely to be different than in the past ~ many more apartments, for instance, or senior citizen dwellings.

Ethno-religious geography

Urban populations are usually organized in such a way that various social groups are residentially segregated from each other. Common bases for sorting are social class, age and ethnicity. In the case of Belfast ethnicity (defined here in terms of Catholics and Protestants) has long been an important feature of life and has found expression in various ways, not least in the form of significant levels of segregation.

New Inner City housing
(Donegall Pass)

As the earlier historical sketch has demonstrated, Belfast was founded by in-comers to Ireland. In consequence, in the early days, the city was a 'Protestant' place. With industrialization in the early nineteenth century, however, there was a large influx of Catholic migrants from rural Ireland. The result was that the Catholic proportion of the population rose to about one-third by mid-century. Thereafter, though Catholic numbers continued to rise, their proportion of the Core City population slowly declined, reaching a low of some 24 percent by 1926. Subsequently the Catholic proportion began to rise again, though absolute numbers declined. By 1991 the Catholic proportion had reached 42 percent, a higher proportion of the Core City population than ever before. Indeed some predictions now suggest a Catholic Core City majority early in the twenty first century. The pattern of proportionate change from the mid-eighteenth century to the present day is shown in Figure 1 on page 13.

Varying proportions of Catholics and Protestants in Belfast's population do not necessarily lead to segregation. However, the growing Catholic population in the nineteenth century appeared to be the trigger for inter-ethnic conflict, with rioting and general commotion punctuating the period from mid-century onwards. This, in turn, sharpened segregation. Figure 7 attempts to show the levels of segregation that have existed from the mid nineteenth century to the present day. What appears to have happened is that relatively tranquil periods, with segregation static or even declining, have been followed by fresh outbursts of inter-communal conflict and sharply increased segregation. This probably occurred in the 1880s, again in the early 1920s, and certainly between 1969 and the mid 1970s. It would seem that each conflict outbreak led to a new and higher segregation level, which then served as the base for further segregation increase during the next period of communal disturbance. Professor Tony Hepburn has referred to this pattern as the *"segregation ratchet."* Several conclusions come from this. Firstly, it seems that Catholic-Protestant segregation in the Core City is higher today than it has ever been. Secondly, it would appear that any decline in segregation during tranquil periods in no significant way counteracts the dramatic increases during the conflict outbursts. From this it would appear that processes that lead to increased segregation are much stronger and have effect much more rapidly than those processes that lead to a reduction in segregated residential patterns. Finally, the *"segregation ratchet"* seems to have operated independently of the absolute numbers of Catholics and Protestants in the Core City, and of their relative proportions.

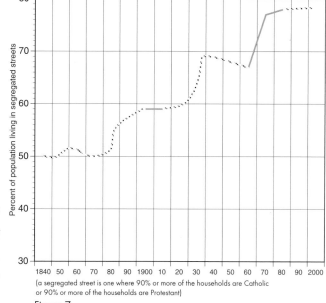

Figure 7
Belfast Core City: The segregation ratchet 1840-1987

(a segregated street is one where 90% or more of the households are Catholic or 90% or more of the households are Protestant)

Estimated levels of segregation

Measured levels of segregation

There is one other aspect of segregation that deserves mention ~ the tendency for the sharp increase that occurred after 1969 to have been particularly concentrated in public sector (social) housing. In early 1969, in the Urban Area, 59 percent of public sector households resided in streets that were completely or almost completely segregated; by 1977 this proportion had risen to 89 percent. For housing in the private sector there was also an increase, but a much more modest one ~ in this case from 65 to 73 percent. Later, when we discuss housing specifically, further comment on this phenomenon will be called for.

Figure 8 shows the distinctive geography of Catholic and Protestant in the Belfast Urban Area. Catholics are particularly concentrated in a large sector that runs south-west from the City Centre. Other clusters occur in the inner north, and part of the inner south and east. Protestants predominate in the intervening spaces, though in many of the more middle-class neighbourhoods there is a substantial Catholic minority population. Segregation, although present both in middle class and working class areas, is particularly sharp in the latter.

Although the ethno-religious distributions have a distinctively sectoral form, there is also a concentric dimension present. While the Core City, in 1991, was 43 percent Catholic, the Urban Area suburbs fell to 22 percent, while the Outer Regional City was only 14 percent Catholic. This, as we will see later, has a profound effect on the nature of residential mobility. Suffice to say here that during the 1970s, while both the Catholic and Protestant inner western parts of the city experienced large scale population loss it was significantly greater in the Protestant areas. Finally, within the Core City alone, the area to the west of the River Lagan is 55 percent Catholic, the area to the east only 12 percent. This means that the terms 'east' and 'west' Belfast have much more than directional significance ~ they are markers of ethnic predominance.

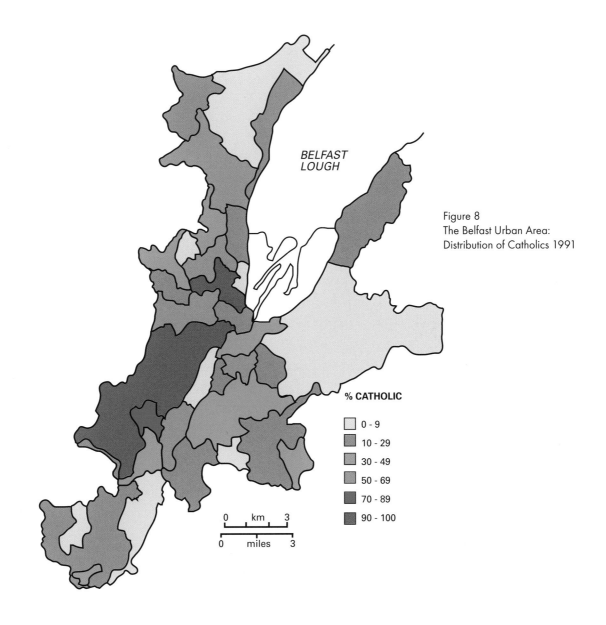

BELFAST
LOUGH

Figure 8
The Belfast Urban Area:
Distribution of Catholics 1991

% CATHOLIC

0 - 9
10 - 29
30 - 49
50 - 69
70 - 89
90 - 100

Young and Old

The Core City can also be explored in terms of its age structure. A number of features can be noted ~ the population, overall, has become older between 1971 and 1991, with the Catholic component in both years being younger than the Protestant.

The ageing population can be seen by comparing the age-sex pyramids for 1971 and 1991. In the former year almost 36 percent of the people in Belfast Core City were under the age of 20 while 12 percent were 65 years of age or older. By 1991 the younger age group had declined to 29 percent while the elderly group had increased to almost 16 percent. It is also worth noting the marked female predominance amongst the oldest section of the population. Moving beyond the city's population as a whole it is evident that there are significant differences in age profiles between the Catholic and the Protestant communities (Figure 9). Thus, 36 percent of Catholics are under the age of 20, this being true for 23 percent of Protestants. Ten percent of Catholics are 65 years of age or older, with 22 percent of Protestants falling into this category. Finally, we can see how these age differentials are found on the ground. The Catholic-Protestant contrast can be seen by comparing the New Lodge (Catholic) and Shankill (Protestant) pyramids. These are two inner city areas that have undergone massive redevelopment.

The varying age compositions of the different groups and areas have major implications for housing and planning, and for social services and educational provision.

As a footnote it is interesting to note the age-sex pyramid for the Botanic Ward. This is an area near Queen's University, and it provides an at least temporary home for a large number of young people, not all of whom are students. In 1991 almost 24 percent of the Core City's population was between 20 and 34 years of age; in Botanic Ward 45 percent were in this age group. It is hardly surprising that the commercial areas nearby throb with activity until the early hours of the morning.

Figure 9a
Belfast Core City Population Pyramids (%)

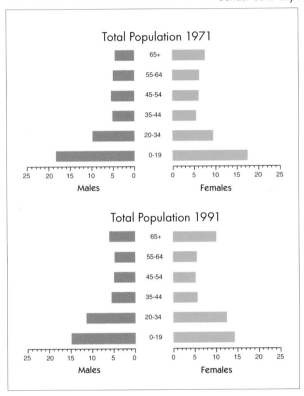

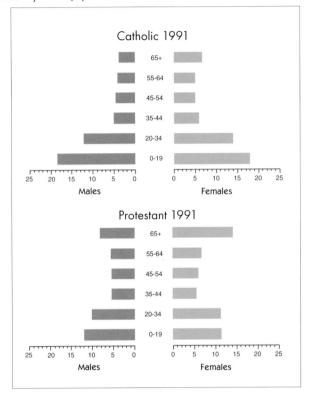

Figure 9b
Pyramids for selected wards 1991 (%)

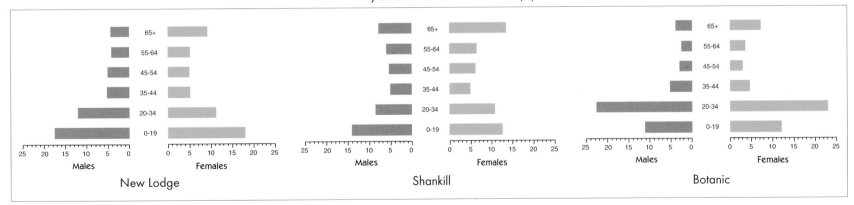

CHAPTER III THE PLANNING EXPERIENCE

Planners have initiated various responses to the dynamics of the city and its region

Late nineteenth century terrace housing

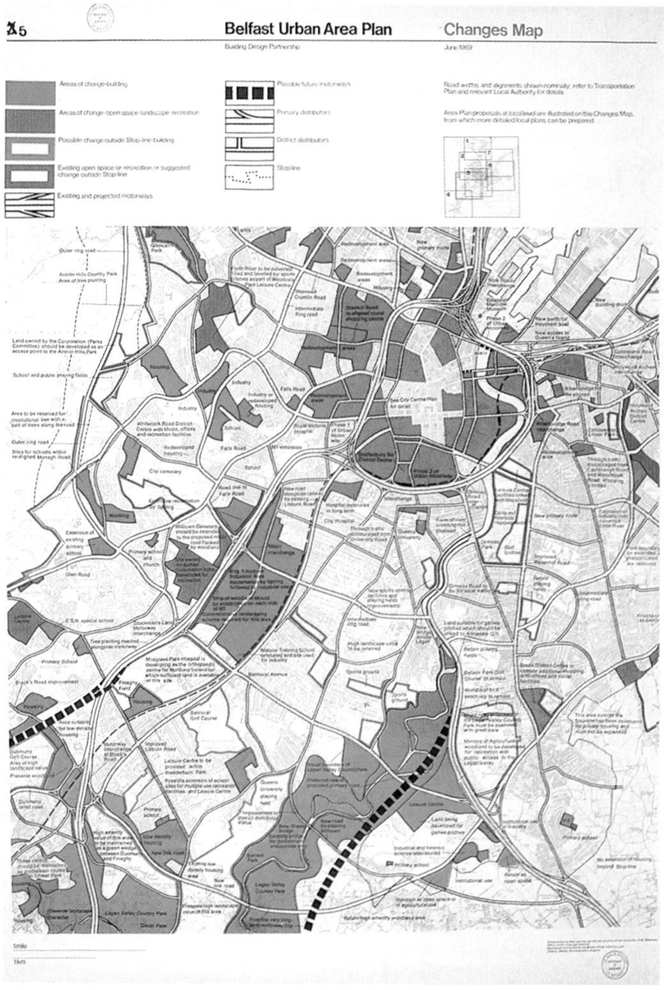

Figure 10
Belfast Urban Area Plan 1969: Central and southern sections

Building Design Partnership

P lanning thinking in Belfast between the end of World War II and the late 1960s was dominated by three basic themes. Firstly, in population and employment terms, Belfast was becoming too big relative to Northern Ireland as a whole. Secondly, the physical spread of the city was threatening to engulf the surrounding hill-slopes and the lush countryside of the Lagan Valley. And thirdly, housing conditions in inner Belfast were deemed to be quite unacceptable, with serious problems of overcrowding and outdated, deteriorated dwellings.

Planning in the 1940s and 1950s.

The planning objectives that have dominated Belfast were given their first public airing in 1942 in a report prepared by W.R. Davidge for the Government of Northern Ireland (Preliminary Report on Reconstruction and Planning). In this, Davidge called both for a plan for the central area and one that would ensure the preservation of a green-belt as a backdrop for the city. One of the bodies set up to implement these proposals, the Planning Commission, presented a series of proposals in 1945 aimed at decentralizing industry and population, whilst also indicating the need to limit the physical extent of the built-up area:

> *With the unfortunate development of English cities in mind, we lay particular stress on the importance of regulating and limiting the outward growth of Belfast, and have therefore carefully scheduled the areas which we believe are most suitable for building development. Outside these areas we strongly recommend that what is commonly known as a 'Green Belt' should be established in which no new buildings except those connected with agriculture, recreation, education or health services should be permitted.*

Housing conditions in the Inner Core City were also a subject for concern. It was noted that much of inner Belfast was characterised by population densities as high as 677 persons/net residential hectare (274 persons/net residential acre) and that it was extremely difficult to provide good living conditions at such densities, particularly with the two storey terrace housing typical of inner Belfast. The Commission indicated that the only solution would be to thin out the high density areas, and rehouse a proportion of their inhabitants elsewhere. The alternative, to build high blocks of flats (apartments) for the whole population of the area was deemed to be unacceptable.

The Planning Commission reiterated these concerns in a further report issued in 1951 ~ Belfast was, relatively, too big and *"all practicable steps should be taken to preserve what remains of the green-belt or agricultural zone."* In addition, the housing problem was reconsidered. It was calculated that some 22,000 new dwellings were needed immediately and that before any large-scale redevelopment could take place in the inner city, there would need to be a steadily increasing outward movement of population in order that decent living conditions could be provided for those who would remain. It was envisaged that the Core City population as a whole should be reduced over time to about 300,000 people. (It will be recalled that by 1951 the population had, in fact, reached 444,000).

In the 1950s, then, there was an acknowledgement of the need to address a number of major planning issues in Belfast and its region. Unfortunately, at this time the planning spirit was willing but the administrative and legislative flesh was weak. Little was done either to limit urban growth or to tackle the physical infrastructure problems of the inner city. Meanwhile, the urban area continued to spread, and while the Core City was beginning to lose population, the continuously built-up area had, by 1961, reached 564,000, this being almost 40 percent of the population of Northern Ireland. Something had to be done.

Planning in the 1960s.

It was in these circumstances that the Northern Ireland Government commissioned Sir Robert Matthew to prepare an advisory plan for the Belfast region. The Regional Plan was published in 1964. The prime objective of the Plan was *"to a modest extent, simultaneously to demagnetize the centre, and re-invigorate the many attractive small towns in the Region."* This was seen as a highly complex conception with two aspects ~ limitation and growth ~ which had to be complementary. Limitation was to be achieved by the imposition of a Stop-line round the Belfast Urban area (See Figure 2). This would not only act to restrict the population growth of the urban area both in absolute terms and relative to that of Northern Ireland as a whole, but would also serve to protect the high amenity areas on the fringe of the built up area. Growth was to be redirected to a number of "centres of development" elsewhere in the region (including Antrim, Ballymena, Bangor, Carrickfergus and Newtownards). The linch pin of the redirected growth policy, however, was to be a new Regional Centre, with the existing towns of Lurgan and Portadown as foci (this new town was later named Craigavon).

Figure 11
The Matthew Regional Plan Strategy 1964

Planning and transportation consultants were subsequently appointed to fill in the details, for the urban area, of Matthew's broad-brush regional scheme. The detailed planning proposals, prepared by Building Design Partnership (BDP), were published in 1969 (a year of enormous significance for Belfast, though little recognized as such at the time). BDP noted that population pressure within the urban area had become even more severe than that observed by Matthew. Indications were that the Matthew BUA target population for 1981 of 600,000, would, in fact be reached as early as 1969, and that if there was only a limited success for the decentralization policy, the urban area population could reach 710,000 by 1986. Unlike Matthew, the BDP plan did take note of the ethnic divisions in the city, recording that *"strong political and religious views were held"* and that *"religion, income and class have marked effects*

Contained by the hills: view across city from Cavehill

upon the demographic structure of the urban area, resulting in an almost complete absence of integrated living between working class Roman Catholics and Protestants." BDP then went on to state that:

> *During our work we have been continuously aware of the strongly held religious and political views which create a very complex social situation. It would be presumptuous, however, to imagine that the Urban Area Plan could be expected to influence religious as well as economic, social and physical factors. Our proposals are designed specifically to facilitate individual and community choice, so that the social patterns desired by the individual and the community may readily be built up.*

Commendable though it be, the facilitation of individual and community choice, when it leads to increased segregation, can be very much a two-edged sword. Not only does it affect general planning, it also becomes a key issue in public sector housing allocation strategies. Finally, while BDP admitted that it would be presumptuous to assume that planning would influence religious (ethnic) issues, they did not consider the possibilities that ethnic factors might, at some point, fundamentally influence plans.

The 1960s plans were oriented to the management of growth ~ how to steer it, how to limit it spatially, while at the same time reducing the population of inner Belfast so that sufficient space could be made available for the provision of housing and other services to a standard much higher than that in the past.

The 1970s Turnaround.

The 1970s was another world altogether. The radical shift in the environment within which planning had to operate is dramatically underlined in a document published by the Department of the Environment in 1977 ~ *Northern Ireland: Regional Physical Development Strategy 1975-1995*. The bottom line, so to speak, was the following:

> *Belfast faces a combination of economic, social, communal and physical development problems unparalleled in any major city in Europe.*

Instead of worrying about growth, extensive decline now became a central concern. As the 1977 strategy document stated:

> *it is clear ... that the whole perspective and tempo of physical planning must undergo a radical reorientation.*

One consequence was that the Stop-line was no longer seen as a mechanism to limit the urban area's population ~ rather it was to serve simply, but importantly, to protect the encompassing hill slopes and the Lagan Valley from urban development.

In the 1970s Belfast was struck by three shock waves ~ demographic, economic and ethnic. Demographically there was a net outflow between 1966 and 1975 of some 76,000 persons, while the birth rate in the Core City dropped by 40 percent. From one perspective, the strategy of thinning the city's population proved to be almost too successful though it did open up an opportunity to raise inner city environmental standards ~ more open spaces, more room for low-rise housing, less, or perhaps no need for residential high rise.

The economic shock, not of course unique to Belfast, made the 1960s, with an unemployment rate of about 5 percent, seem like boom times. The 1977 Strategy document noted that unemployment was currently running at 10 percent and that the economic outlook was overshadowed by problems of regional peripherality, overdependence on industries whose labour requirements were declining, lack of employment opportunities, civil unrest and a generally depressed investment climate in the advanced economies as a whole. Indeed, the economic shock of the 1970s sharpened in intensity through the early 1980s producing, by 1986, an unemployment rate of some 20 percent in the Urban Area, with pockets of male unemployment as high as 50 percent.

Last, but by no means least, a renewed outburst of violent ethnic conflict in 1969, which continued for the following 25 years, provided a further jolt to the urban system and to extant planning strategies. Ethnic residential segregation increased sharply, many households were forced or perceived the need to relocate. Housing abandonment affected neighbourhoods on or near ethnic interfaces, while much damage was caused to the commercial and residential fabric of the city by terrorist action. Thus the ethnic shock compounded the economic and demographic perturbations.

Scorched earth: Farringdon Gardens - fire and flight August 1971

Safety first

Scorched earth: Farringdon Gardens - the morning after

The most recent major planning exercise for Belfast is *The Belfast Urban Area Plan 2001*, published for discussion in 1987 and in final form in 1990. Here we get a fresh set of signals ~ more modest than the 1960s schemes, more optimistic than those of the 1977 Strategy document.

There have been signs of recovery during the first half of the 1980s as reflected in the decline in the rate of outward migration, the growth in the total number of households in the Urban Area and a strong inward flow of public and private investment.

The objective of the 2001 Plan is to gently build on these encouraging manifestations of recovery. A small growth in the Urban Area population by 2001 is rather tentatively indicated, to be mainly accommodated in proposed housing areas on the edge of the Green Belt. Now, the Matthew Plan Stop-line becomes a more flexible instrument for the controlled release of urban edge land. Undoubtedly, the evidence of the 1991 census, which postdates the plan, gives guarded encouragement to these predictions of modest growth.

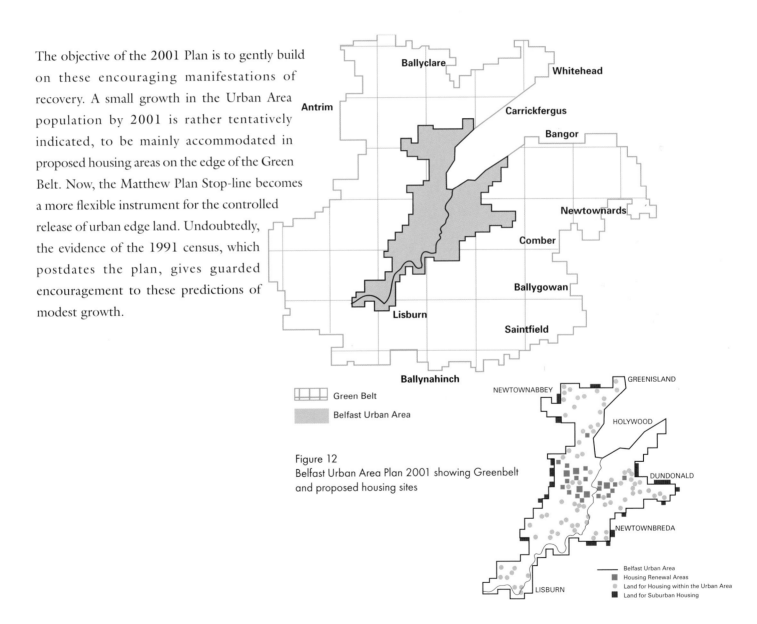

Figure 12
Belfast Urban Area Plan 2001 showing Greenbelt and proposed housing sites

CHAPTER IV HOUSING THE PEOPLE

In recent years, the provision of public sector dwellings in Belfast has been quite revolutionary in its impact on housing quality and the appearance of the city

Inner City Redevelopment: Sandy Row

Pound Loney: Divis area before redevelopment

When Building Design Partnership published their plan for the Belfast Urban Area in 1969, they estimated that 74,500 new dwellings would be required ~ the demand coming from the removal of unfit housing, from the consequence of motorway route clearance programmes and from new household formation. About a third of these would have to be provided beyond the Urban Area (in the Outer Regional City and in the Matthew designated growth towns beyond). Between 15 and 20 percent of the new dwellings to be provided in the Urban Area itself would need to be high-rise (above 4 or 5 storeys).

Renewal

Effective redevelopment of poor quality inner city housing stock had been very slow to get started in Belfast. The first redevelopment area was designated in 1962, but the programme only really got underway in the late 1960s. A number of tower blocks were built, some in the inner city, some in suburban locations. In addition, a major complex of eight storey deck - access blocks was constructed at the inner city end of the Falls Road sector, (later known as Divis Flats). All this saw Belfast rather belatedly trying to catch up with cities in Britain, where redevelopment had progressed much further, and where high rise solutions were the flavour of the month. With hindsight, Belfast's lagardliness turned out to be a blessing, as many of the deck access and maisonette units proved very unpopular with residents. Indeed, most of these have now been demolished, being replaced with much more traditional (but high quality) two and three storey terraces.

Divis Flats: The 1960s solution

Divis Flats: The 1990s response - from deck access to traditional terrace

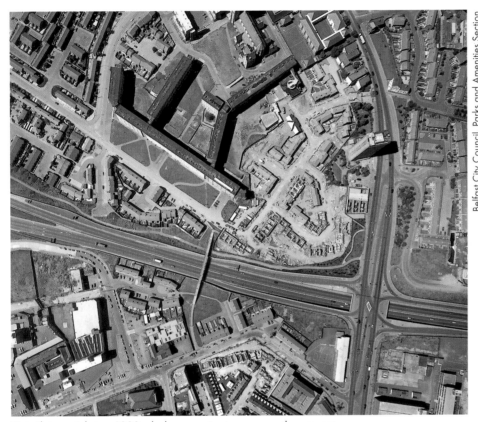

Belfast City Council, Parks and Amenities Section

Divis Flats: aerial view 1990 - deck access structures are on the way out

The new Divis

Demolition on the Shankill: The "Weetabix boxes" go

Up to 1971, social housing provision was the responsibility of the various local government units, aided substantially by the contribution of the Northern Ireland Housing Trust. By this time, the political scene was becoming fraught with inter-ethnic violence rapidly escalating. Partly in response to concerns about fairness in public sector housing provision, and partly due to a wish to create a more efficient mechanism for social housing production, the Government of Northern Ireland created the Northern Ireland Housing Executive.

This body took over the functions of all the existing social housing bodies. However its remit extended beyond the public sector ~ it was also called upon to help the private sector, to monitor housing conditions, to undertake housing research programmes and to provide housing advice and information. In the Belfast Urban Area, the Executive became responsible for a variety of pre-existing schemes, developing its own programme in subsequent years.

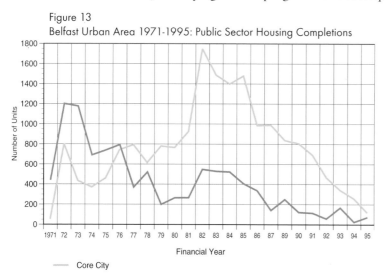

Figure 13
Belfast Urban Area 1971-1995: Public Sector Housing Completions

Number of Units

Financial Year

Core City

Urban Area
Suburbs

The first House Condition Survey, carried out in 1974, showed that 24 percent of the dwellings in the Core City were unfit. It also demonstrated that housing conditions in Belfast were the worst in any major city in the United Kingdom. A significant component of the building programme in the early and mid 1970s involved construction on green-field sites on the edge of the urban area. From 1977 onwards, however, there was a radical shift of emphasis, with the bulk

Inner City New Build:
Shankill Redevelopment

of construction being concentrated in the inner city. As Figure 13 shows, this focus became sharply accentuated in the 1980s, the first half of the decade producing almost 8,500 completions, three-quarters of which were in the Core City. By 1979 Core City dwelling unfitness had dropped to 15 percent; this figure further declined to about 11 percent by 1987, decreasing to 8 percent by 1991.

Public Sector in the Suburbs: Rathcoole, Newtownabbey

Now its mine! Public Sector House Sales

Co-Ownership Housing

Chapelfields Fold: Inner City Housing
Association development

The massive public sector new build programme has radically transformed the physical fabric of inner Belfast. It has also contributed fundamentally to changing the pattern of dwelling tenure (Figure 14). Most notable has been the very large decline in dwellings rented in the private sector, balanced by a steady rise in both owner occupation and social housing. In 1961 about 14 percent of dwellings were in the public sector; by 1991 this had reached one third. Of course, the Inner City saw the greatest change, as much mainly unfit private rented property was compulsorily purchased and subsequently redeveloped as social housing. The increase in owner occupation on the other hand, is partly due to the combined impacts of the Housing Executive's Voluntary House Sales Scheme and the part rent/part buy programme operated by the Northern Ireland Co-Ownership Housing Association Ltd. Indeed, it is striking to note that over the period 1980-93 more owner-occupied stock was added in the Core City by the Voluntary Sales Scheme than by the totality of private sector new build. Together, public sector sales and co-ownership have helped many households onto what they hope will be the first rung of the home ownership ladder.

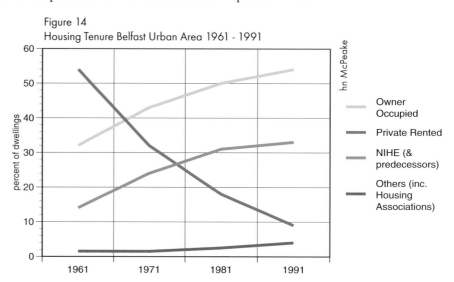

Figure 14
Housing Tenure Belfast Urban Area 1961 - 1991

Ian McPeake

Owner Occupied

Private Rented

NIHE (& predecessors)

Others (inc. Housing Associations)

Waiting for the Bulldozer - and a better future

Partnership in urban renewal is strongly reflected in the work of the Housing Association movement in the city. Housing Associations have played a valuable complementary role to the Housing Executive's renewal programme, and since the early 1970s have built or rehabilitated approximately 6,500 homes in the Core City.

The contributions made by the various housing bodies and the private sector to Belfast's renewal and expansion over recent years have been highly variable, both in volume and in area of impact. If we compare the Core City with the Regional City as a whole, for the period 1979-93, we find that over 60 percent of Housing Association dwellings were constructed in the Core City; for the Housing

Inner City Renewal: Donegall Pass

Executive this rises to almost 70 percent. Thus, over the 14 year period, about two-thirds of social housing new build took place in the Core City; in marked contrast only 14 percent of private sector dwellings were built there. Private sector new build, thus, is a phenomenon of the Urban Area suburbs and of the Outer Regional City, presumably reflecting both the pattern of demand and the availability of sites. Renewal, basically, has been a public sector phenomenon; expansion, predominantly, a private sector initiative.

Inner city transformation, necessarily backed as it was by major government financial subvention, has been a remarkable phenomenon in many ways. Not only was the quality of the housing stock greatly improved, but the replacement dwellings were constructed to conform to what residents desired ~ two storey houses in short terraces, not tower blocks, maisonettes or (horror of horrors) deck access structures! All this was achieved in a highly unfavourable environment ~ violent communal conflict, extreme rigidities in people's willingness to be rehoused anywhere but within the perceived security of their own ethnic communities, evidence of paramilitary involvement in organized squatting and in extortion rackets etc. The fact, as noted earlier, that the highest levels of ethnic segregation are found in public sector housing is, therefore, not to be explained by any intention on the part of the Housing Executive to create or maintain such separation. Rather, it is due to the Executive responding to the demands, from many applicants, for housing allocations in "safe" territory.

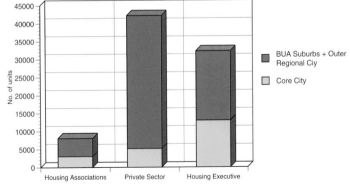

Fig 15
Belfast Regional City 1979 -93: Housing starts and housing providers

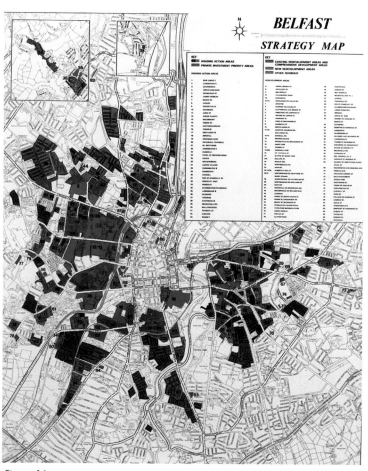

Figure 16
Belfast Housing Renewal Strategy 1982

The key document of this period was Belfast: Housing Renewal Strategy produced by the Housing Executive in 1982. Affecting some 27,000 dwellings, replacement and rehabilitation were seen as the key elements of the renewal strategy. The Strategy Map (Figure 16) highlights several features ~ the massive extent of the programme, and the mix of approaches to be adopted. As can be seen there was an inner ring where clearance and redevelopment was the technique, surrounded by an outer band where rehabilitation would be dominant. To achieve the latter objective Housing Action Areas were designated, these being characterized by a high level of housing stress, but where conditions still favoured the retention and modernization of dwellings. This work was carried out by the Housing Executive, Housing Associations or private individuals. Rehabilitation rather than renewal was favoured by many affected communities, as it was judged to be much less socially disruptive. There was concern, however, that some rehabilitation work was costing almost as much as a new dwelling, while the useful life-span of the product was significantly shorter. In addition, as residents began to see the results of the 1980s new build programme, satisfaction regarding the older rehabilitated stock decreased.

Expansion

New Life for Old Stock - The Housing Action Area approach

The third strand to the housing renewal strategy was the PIPA's (Private Investment Priority Areas). In the early 1980s it was established that 16,800 dwellings in the Core City, while outside the scope of the redevelopment and Housing Action Areas strategies, were in need of comprehensive improvement. Here the objective was to stem the spread of disrepair in the ring outside the redevelopment heartland. It was hoped that young and economically active people could be encouraged to acquire, repair and improve their homes by use of grants and Building Society support. While achieving some success, the PIPA programme has demonstrated the difficulties of tackling unfitness where it affects a rather scattered collection of individual or small clusters of dwellings, and where the willingness and ability of residents to involve themselves in such action is itself a highly variable phenomenon. As a result, PIPAs have now given way to Housing Action Areas which cover 20,000 properties in 47 areas. The new Renovation Grants Scheme, introduced in 1992, is designed to target aid at unfit properties, with the amount of grant payable determined by the result of a test of the applicant's financial resources.

Without question, the housing revolution has been most evident in the inner city. Suburban public sector development has been much less extensive, over the past 20 years, as energies turned to redevelopment rather than overspill. Suburban private sector housing expansion within the BUA has also been limited, due, to a considerable extent, to the land supply constraints imposed by the

1960s Private Sector Suburbia

Stop-line. However, since 1974, there has been, a certain amount of Stop-line nibbling as the development limit became not so much a complete barrier to the spread of the built-up area as a device for controlled release of building sites. In particular, two quite dramatic changes to the urban limit were approved - Poleglass on the south-western edge of the city and Cairnshill on the south-east. The former was in response to the demand for public sector accommodation in the south-west (Falls/Andersonstown) segment of the city. This demand was literally corked up by the constraining presence of Protestant territory, particularly evident to the north and south east within the Core City. Pressure could only be relieved by permitting a Stop-line extension at the outer south-west end of the Catholic concentration. Thus the territorial inelasticities of Belfast fundamentally shaped the expansion of the urban area. These inelasticities were given stark expression and, indeed, were reinforced by the construction of the so-called Peace Lines, now located at 16 Catholic - Protestant interfaces. (Figure 17)

Development commenced at Poleglass in 1979, amidst considerable political controversy and a further expansion, in the same area at Lagmore, is now well underway. The Protestant Shankill, in contrast to the Falls, did not generate a significant demand for new housing provision at the urban edge. This contrast was due to Protestant-Catholic demographic differentials, together with the wider range of suburban housing opportunities that were territorially acceptable to Protestants. Of course there was also the coincidental effect of topography ~ the Catholic Falls sector is oriented outwards towards the relatively subdued topography of the lower slopes of the Lagan Valley; the Protestant Shankill dead-ends against the extremely steep hill edge to the north-west of the Urban Area.

Belfast City Council, Parks and Amenities Section

The Poleglass Development

Claiming space and proclaiming the message

The daddy of them all - the Cupar Street Wall

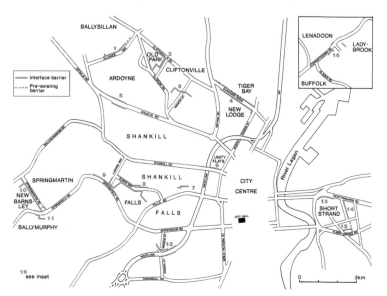

Figure 17
The Belfast "Peace Lines" 1994

Dividing space - the Cupar Street view from the air 1990
(line of wall highlighted in red)

BCC, Parks and Amenities Section

Peace walls become "Environmental Barriers": Alliance Avenue

The narrow ground - peace line in east Belfast

Beyond the Stop Line: Cairnshill on the march

Cairnshill is quite a different story. Here, pressure came from the private sector due to shortage of sites for the construction of owner occupied dwellings. In the south-east segment some of the gentler hill-slopes had already succumbed to a red-brick tide by the late 1950s. The Cairnshill extension did not further violate the sharply defined topographic edge of the city ~ rather, it added a significant increment to the urban flood that had already breached the dyke.

Poleglass and Cairnshill, as peripheral expansions that broke the Stop-line, pinpoint the delicately balanced nature of the planning strategy for the Belfast Urban Area. Back at the time of the Urban Area Plan of the late 1960s, concern was expressed that the Stop-line should not be breached ~ otherwise the proposed growth centres in the Outer Regional City and beyond would be weakened to the point where they would be unable to contribute to the solution of the then existing problems of the city. Today concern still focuses on the extent to which the Stop-line will limit urban expansion ~ but now the fear is that, if too little land is released, people may move out of the BUA altogether. This outcome, of course, was precisely the objective of the 1960s planners! There is a final twist to all this ~ too much land released for private sector housing development at the periphery of the Urban Area may weaken the impact of the inner city reinvigoration strategy, and may additionally weaken housing demand in a number of Housing Executive (mainly Protestant) estates, causing an increase in vacant property and a selective out-migration. This would result in neighbourhoods increasingly characterized by elderly residents, single-parent families and so on. It is obviously very difficult ~ if wellnigh impossible ~ to get the urban limitation exercise exactly right.

Chapter V In and Out of Work

In a recent strategy document issued by the Making Belfast Work initiative it is claimed that "Belfast cannot work if its people do not."
While community conflict and its associated violence has been a dominant theme in Belfast over the past 25 years, so has unemployment.

Lunchbreak

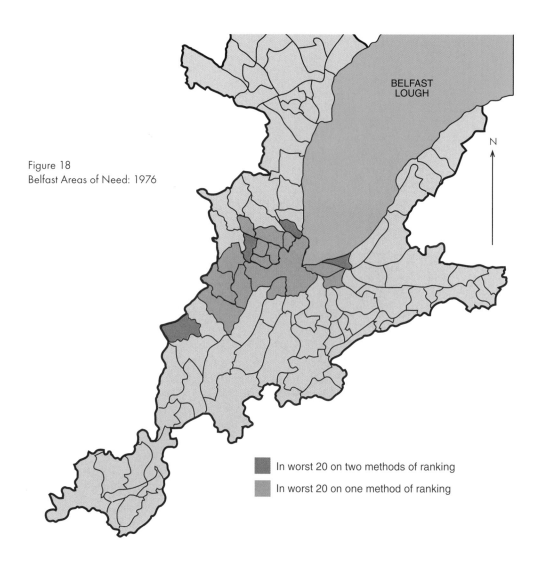

Figure 18
Belfast Areas of Need: 1976

BELFAST
LOUGH

N

In worst 20 on two methods of ranking
In worst 20 on one method of ranking

The planning publications produced in the 1960s made some reference to unemployment levels and the need to ameliorate the problem. The 1969 Belfast Urban Area Plan recorded an unemployment rate for 1968 of five percent. By 1972 this had grown to eight percent, followed by a rapid rise to 21 percent by 1981. Thus, just as the 1970s saw a sharp increase in residential segregation, so the same decade was one of markedly increased unemployment. Through the 1980s unemployment remained stubbornly stuck at slightly less than 20 percent. Indeed, pockets of unemployment existed where over half the workforce had no job. These pockets have been particularly concentrated in the inner city and in the western sector, representing great social inequality (in 1991 the worst ward for unemployment had a rate of 50 percent, the best ward 3 percent!). The rapid rise in unemployment through the 1970s and its continued existence at a high level in the 1980s became another factor steering policy making away from the 1960s concerns about excessive growth. Moreover, reports on studies of social need began to appear (Figure 18) leading to the delimitation of areas of special social need and the direction of additional   government funding to those same areas.

These early studies were updated in the 1980s and most recently by using data derived from the 1991 census (Figure 19). Every analysis since 1974 has shown almost exactly the same pattern - a concentration of disadvantage in the inner city and in a sector to the west. Bluntly, there has been much mapping but not much success at ameliorating the problems (except in so far as they are housing related). One is reminded of Professor David Harvey's 1973 comment that ... *mapping even more evidence of man's potent inhumanity to man is counter revolutionary in the sense that it allows the bleeding-heart liberal in us to pretend we are contributing to a solution when in fact we are not.*

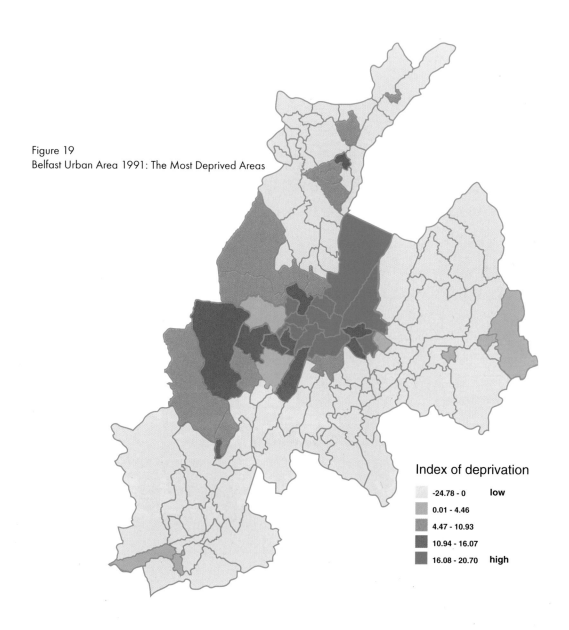

Figure 19
Belfast Urban Area 1991: The Most Deprived Areas

Index of deprivation

-24.78 - 0   **low**

0.01 - 4.46

4.47 - 10.93

10.94 - 16.07

16.08 - 20.70   **high**

On the other hand, the view expressed almost 150 years ago by the Belfast clergyman, Rev. William Murphy O'Hanlon is worth noting - *it is my intention, by the Divine blessing, to extend my walks and enquiries to several quarters of the town; and, if the public will listen, to note and describe some of the evils which exist in our midst - hoping that the attempt may issue in the origination of some further schemes of amelioration, or in the more vigorous working of those already in existence.*

The 1970s Belfast Areas of Need (BAN) study provided a basis for focusing additional resources on the most deprived locations. Recently the Making Belfast Work (MBW) project has emerged to assist in the task. Since 1988 MBW has been working to strengthen and target more effectively the efforts being made by local communities, by the private sector and by the government, to address the economic, educational, social, health and environmental problems associated with living in the most disadvantaged areas of Belfast. The MBW area of operation (Figure 20) is highly coincident with those areas depicted as deprived in the earlier studies. This coincidence undoubtedly underlines the stubbornness of the problems confronted - despite the allocation of an additional £150 million to 150 projects over the past six years. Poverty lies at the root of many of the problems and unemployment lies at the root of much of the poverty. However, MBW is aware that

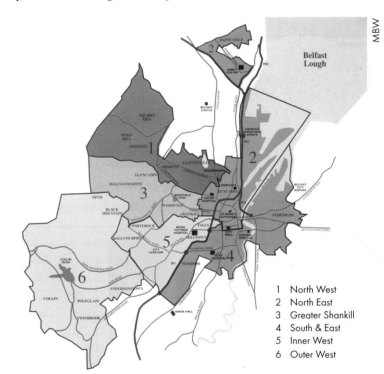

1 North West
2 North East
3 Greater Shankill
4 South & East
5 Inner West
6 Outer West

Figure 20
Making Belfast Work Areas 1995

creating sufficient new jobs is an uphill task ~ "it is hard to see a quick and easy route to full and fulfilling employment when, in the European Union, unemployment hovers around 17 million."

Since the 1960s many jobs in manufacturing have been lost ~ in textiles, engineering and in shipbuilding (the core industries of Belfast's late Victorian industrial boom). Attempts were made to find substitutes, for instance synthetic fibres or the unhappy Delorean car manufacturing venture. Recently government has developed a strategy that attempts to encourage small community based enterprises. This has its own irony, since much of the large scale urban renewal projects of the 1960s and early 1970s swept away a great deal of back alley businesses. This is dramatically illustrated by what happened in the Shankill area. Here, 200 small businesses present in 1968 had been reduced to 11 by 1983, and 202 corner shops had shrunk to one. Recently, as a counter to this, clusters of small business units (BUNS) have been constructed in the inner city to provide modern, appropriately sized buildings for occupation by new enterprises.

Enterprise Zone accessability

Another strategy aimed at job creation has been the designation of an Enterprise Zone. This began in 1981 and consisted of 2 sections ~ 77 hectares (190 acres) on reclaimed land in the harbour area, and a further 132 hectares (325 acres) in the western part of the inner city (Figure 21). The Enterprise Zone was aimed at encouraging private business to start up or expand by offering a whole range of incentives such as rate exemption for 10 years from 1981, tax allowances for capital expenditure, and a greatly relaxed planning scheme. By 1986, 6,000 jobs had been located in the Enterprise Zone, though less than half of these were new, the rest being relocations. Thirty percent of the new jobs were in manufacturing, the remainder in services.

Enterprise Zone: in the Harbour Section

Figure 21
The Belfast Enterprise Zone

The harbour section of the Enterprise Zone has been much more successful than that in the inner city, the latter being a less attractive environment and with transportation facilities that compare unfavourably. Indeed it may be significant that a proposal has recently been tabled for a new University of Ulster campus on former inner city Enterprise Zone land (Springvale). Perhaps the mega-employment creation projects of the future are not to be in manufacturing but in services? While such a scheme should improve educational opportunities in the deprived West Belfast area, there is a major question as to just how many jobs will be created for local people.

The Decline in Manufacturing: Part of the shipyard

The ethnically fractured geography of the Belfast Urban Area has been an obstacle to labour mobility, as there has been a reluctance at times to travel to work in the other side's territory. The more peaceful conditions evident in 1995 should lead to a loosening of this constraint.

When we look at the patterns of employment in the Belfast Urban Area over the past three decades, a number of very striking features becomes evident. First, contrary to general impression, there are just about as many jobs in the area now as there were in the early 1970s (around 220,000). Secondly, and this time in line with general expectations, there has been a radical shift in the balance between manufacturing employment and that in services (Figure 22). While in 1971 almost 40 percent of the jobs were in manufacturing, this had dropped by 1985 to about 25 percent and by 1993 to only 16 percent. At the same time the burgeoning service sector was itself becoming increasingly characterized by a growth in public sector jobs (administration, security etc.). Thirdly, there has been a significant shift in the location of the employment. In 1966 the City Centre and the Inner City had approximately two thirds of the jobs; fifteen years later, in 1981, this had declined to slightly less than half.

Thus Belfast has seen a curious paradox ~ a fairly constant number of jobs located within the BUA, together with a large increase in unemployment. Explanation lies in a number of changes that have taken place. Firstly, a much higher proportion of the jobs in inner Belfast are

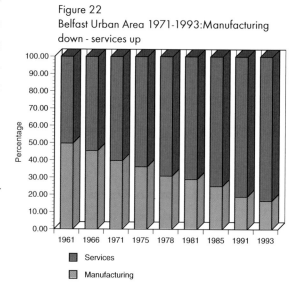

Figure 22
Belfast Urban Area 1971-1993:Manufacturing down - services up

■ Services

□ Manufacturing

now held by workers who commute from beyond the Core City (in many instances from beyond the BUA itself). Thus, by way of illustration, it can be noted that in 1971, 37 percent of Core City jobs were filled by commuters. By 1991 this had risen to 53 percent. Significantly, there was no compensating increase in the flow of Core City residents to jobs beyond the city boundary. Secondly, a higher proportion of the population now seeks employment, with a particularly marked increase in the number of females entering the job market. While older, predominantly male, workers have been made redundant by contraction in manufacturing industry and have consequently borne a disproportionate share of the increased unemployment, this has been even more the case for young people coming onto the job market for the first time. Thus, the highest rates of unemployment are to be found amongst those under the age of 30. It is also interesting to note that over the past decade males have steadily become a greater proportion of the unemployed in the Urban Area (2.75 males to every female in 1987; 3.66 males to every female in 1995).

Just as the past three decades have seen a dramatic restructuring both of the built environment and of population distribution in Belfast Regional City, so the same can be said for employment. However, it seems, even after noting all the difficulties associated with physical planning, that response to change in the physical fabric of the city has been considerably more successful than response to change in employment. Perhaps, in the latter case, the forces at work are much too powerful for any local tinkering to have much more than a palliative effect. In the era of automation and information technology, many people need to find sources of income that provide an alternative to either traditional paid employment or to welfare payments.

New houses - Yes! New jobs?

Chapter VI Special Places

Cities are made-up of special places - city centres, neighbourhoods, parks, and so on.
Here we look at two such places - the Lagan Corridor and the City Centre

City centre and river

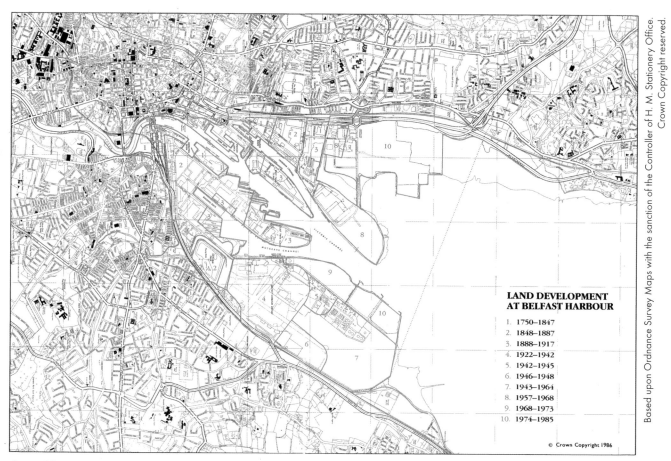

LAND DEVELOPMENT
AT BELFAST HARBOUR

1. 1750–1847
2. 1848–1887
3. 1888–1917
4. 1922–1942
5. 1942–1945
6. 1946–1948
7. 1943–1964
8. 1957–1968
9. 1968–1973
10. 1974–1985

© Crown Copyright 1986

Figure 23
Filling the lough: Reclamation 1750-1985

The Lagan Corridor

A study of the river, published in 1978 claimed that "the Lagan is synonymous with Belfast; Belfast with the Lagan." And yet, a curious ambiguity surrounds the city's relationship with its river. The early crossing point certainly set the town's location in general terms, but the initial settlement grew, not on the Lagan, but on a small left bank tributary, the Farset. Again, as nineteenth century urbanization occurred, the inner part of the city virtually turned its back on the Lagan, seeing it not as a focus, but as something to be ignored, or at most used as a convenience for moving certain commodities, for extracting water or depositing waste. Further upstream, the growing city virtually avoided the river, with, in this case, very positive long term consequences.

Only at the mouth of the Lagan could Belfast and the river really be said to have combined fruitfully; here the port developed, together with large concentrations of industrial activity.

The Lagan Corridor is made up of three distinctive segments ~ the downstream port complex, the middle urban stretch, and the upstream rural zone.

The Port

The port has been a key component in Belfast's growth. It has formed, from the beginning, a vital entry and exit point for people and commodities. It has also provided the site for one of Belfast's focal activities ~ shipbuilding ~ as well as for a wide range of other industry. At the port, Belfast has reached out not only in its trading activities, but physically. It was almost as if the Lagan was too short for the city, for to a quite remarkable degree reclamation and channel cutting and deepening have combined

Where once the Lough: Dargan landfill, Victoria Terminals and the Belfast City Airport

to stretch the river in a downstream direction. The low-lying, tidal mud-flats at the head of Belfast Lough both created the need and provided the opportunity to claim large areas from the sea. (Figure 23) In 1960 Emrys Jones described things thus:

> *Gradual though the work has been over the last century or so, its cumulative effect has been to effect a major change in the landscape, a change which has been emphasized by the use made of this new land. It forms a quadrant of industrial land, where grain elevators and storage sheds, gantrys and engineering works, have quite transformed the tidal strands which once bordered the Lough.*

Since Jones wrote this, the reclaimed area has expanded by a further 80 percent. By 1985 the total reclaimed zone covered some 720 hectares (1779 acres). Perhaps only now are there signs of a halt being called to all this as concerns about environmental impact come to the fore. The loss of the mud-flats has greatly reduced the availability of feeding grounds for many species of birds. Indeed some of the more recent landfill itself is not now seen as providing opportunities for urban development. Rather, it is being designated as open space and, more specifically, in some cases, as nature reserve.

As further land has been reclaimed, particularly since World War II, so technological change has pulled port activity to the wide open spaces and deeper channels downstream. The widespread use of roll-on/roll-off goods transfer, together with the lift-on/lift-off of unit loads (containers) have called for quite different harbour configurations than in the past. Large areas for handling containers are now required and these are most readily found on the outward stretches of the reclamation zone. The Victoria Terminals are the prime examples of this development. The migration of port activity downstream, a world-wide phenomenon, has, however, opened new opportunities further upstream.

Queen's University

Victoria Terminals: Container port and roll - on/roll - off terminal

Technological change in the port area has also been strikingly evident with shipbuilding. While overall production levels at Harland and Wolff have declined markedly, construction methods have shifted from the slipways to the building dock. The consequent float out is much less dramatic than the earlier slip launch, but the scale of the production facilities, certainly in terms of visual impact, provides compensation. While shipyard gantries used to dominate the Lagan's lower reaches, now the most striking symbolic and functional structures in the city are the two huge, yellow cranes hovering over the building dock.

The reclaimed land on the south-east side of the estuary has also provided extensive sites for the development of aircraft manufacturing, carried out by Shorts, now a subsidiary of the Quebec company, Bombardier. The associated airstrip has evolved to become the Belfast City Airport, handling a large volume of mainly short-haul flights to and from mainland UK locations. The airport is a highly convenient facility, being sited a mere four kilometres (two and a quarter miles) from the city centre. Unfortunately convenience for some has been obtained at the price of increased noise pollution for others.

Victoria Terminals: Containerization

Esler Crawford

Laganside: The big picture

The Middle River

Upstream from the docks, the river was bordered by a considerable variety of urban structures and functions ~ factories, bus depots, livestock and fruit and vegetable markets, a gas works, and various bits and pieces of nineteenth century inner city housing. Belfast, in this section, has historically turned a rather ugly back on the river.

Some early efforts at improvement took place, albeit in that part of the river edge upstream from the most intensively urbanized section. This work was instigated by the 1924 Act which granted the city government powers to undertake the construction of a weir and to improve embankments. Concern about the quality of the river itself and of its immediate environs was expressed in the 1969 Urban Area Plan, but a focussed assault on the river and its 'problems' can most properly be dated from 1978, when the River Lagan government working party tabled a wide-ranging set of proposals for improvement. Following this a Concept Plan for the Urban Lagan was prepared by consultants and issued in 1987. Fundamental change was finally placed in motion in 1989 with the creation of the Laganside Corporation. This sharply focussed, limited life body, was mandated to secure the regeneration of its designated area, a stretch of the river basically between the upstream end of the harbour and the point (at Stranmillis) where the river loses its urban accoutrements. (Figure 24). The scene for its activities was set by the 1987 Concept Plan:

Cities throughout Europe and North America are rediscovering their waterfronts. Whilst Belfast has a rich maritime tradition, it yet has to realize the development opportunities offered by re-uniting buildings and space with water. The Lagan could become one of the most attractive rivers in Europe.

Laganside: The Gasworks site, river and Ormeau Park beyond

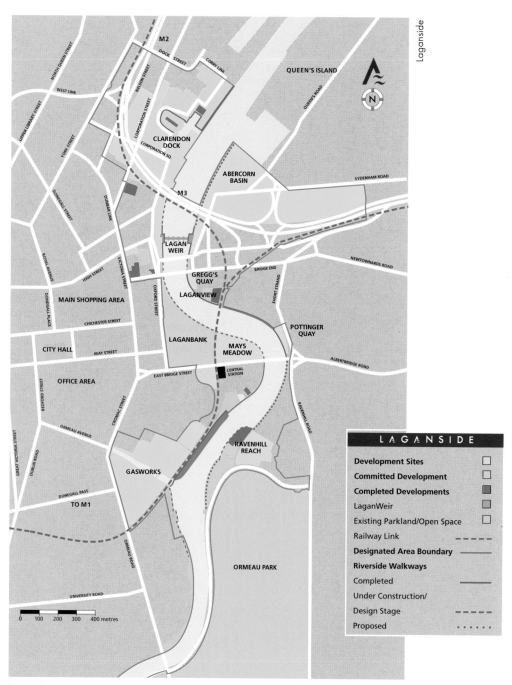

Figure 24
Laganside: The Designated Area

The Laganside Corporation was granted powers to undertake physical works, to acquire and dispose of land, to enter into agreements for the development of land, to offer appropriate financial assistance for such developments and to make bye-laws to control the use of the river itself within the designated area.

The creation of an attractive riverside environment was aimed not only at drawing in private sector commercial functions, but also at ensuring that housing and social and recreational facilities would be available to encourage people to live and work in the area.

The Corporation's focus has been on infrastructural activity. The linch-pin of the whole river improvement exercise is the Lagan Weir, completed in 1994. This helps maintain a constant high water level upstream, avoiding the daily emergence of unsightly mud-banks at low tide. In addition it is designed to reduce the tendency of the ponded river to stratification ~ an undesirable outcome whereby dense salt water sinks to the bottom of the riverbed creating an oxygen-starved environment. In addition to the new weir a major programme of dredging has been completed, to improve water quality and depth and also the appearance of the river. Of interest is the fact that much of the dredged material has contributed to reclamation in the harbour area.

Laganside: Weir, cross-harbour railbridge, shipyard cranes beyond

Laganside: Reflections

Laganside: Waterfront Hall June 1995

River walkways have been constructed and site works carried out on a number of key locations, where substantial land has become available as a consequence of the closure of certain functions (Gasworks and markets) or the downstream movement of elements of the port function. Clarendon Dock is an example of the latter, while Laganbank and the Gasworks site fall under the former. One might argue that Laganbank is the most crucial of all the activity. The site presents, in many ways, direct continuity between the City Centre and the river. A large 2,235 seat concert and conference hall (the Waterfront Hall) is the most dramatic manifestation of this development to date.

Finally, new residential development is being introduced to the riverbank. This has definitely not been a feature of Belfast life to date, but demand indicates that there is a market for centre city river-front accommodation. The only fear, expressed by some, is that there is a risk of disassociation between new up-market/yuppie dwellers on the river and deprived, inner city neighbourhoods nearby.

Laganside: Riverfront living

The Regional Park

The third component of the Lagan Corridor is the Regional Park. As the city spread south-westwards between the Antrim and Down hills, it tended to diverge away from the river. The main roads sought routes that at one and the same time avoided both low lying, floodable terrain and the topographic jumble through which the river makes its way. Thus, with great good fortune, the river valley upstream has avoided most of the urbanization that created both problem and opportunity for the Laganside Corporation. A relatively pristine rural scene survived, with only occasional markers of nineteenth century industrialization to disrupt the idyll (linen mills and the manifestations of a canal system).

Lagan Valley Regional Park: The river at Minnowburn

The Matthew Regional Plan of 1964 made reference to the notable visual qualities of the Lagan between Belfast and Lisburn, calling, amongst other things for the prevention of any further intrusive urban development. In preparing the Belfast Urban Area Plan, Building Design Partnership presented a report on *The Lagan Valley Country Park (1967)*. In this they called for the establishment of a park, developed for recreation and landscape purposes ~ in a situation where the recreational potential of the valley was almost completely undeveloped and its landscape value increasingly threatened by inappropriate development. The park area (originally limited to the area that could be seen from the old canal towpath) was given some general protection in 1965 when the encompassing land was designated an Area of Outstanding Natural Beauty.

Following the adoption of the Belfast Urban Area Plan 2001 (in 1990) a local plan was prepared for what is now referred to as the Regional Park. (Figure 25). This plan was issued in 1993, confirming the Park as an area of special scenic character and recreational potential, to be protected and

Lagan Valley Regional Park: Relaxation in the city?

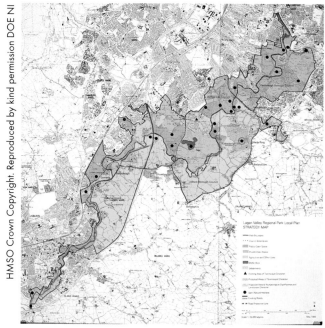

HMSO Crown Copyright. Reproduced by kind permission DOE NI

Figure 25
Lagan Valley Regional Park: Local Plan

enhanced. The designated area now extends to 1700 hectares (4,200 acres), forming a narrow, riverine strip along some 21 kilometres (13 miles) of river. Gradually access to the park has been improved and internal pathways developed. A significant portion of the land is in public ownership; the remaining private space serves to provide a protected frame.

The Lagan Corridor, stretching from the estuarine lands at the head of Belfast Lough, through the highly developed landscapes of the harbour, shipyard and inner city to the open, riverside above and then to the strikingly rural Regional Park, provides a growing focus for the whole Urban Area, a focus being greatly enhanced by actions taken over the past three decades, most evident today in the drama of Laganside.

The City Centre

City Hall with retail core beyond

Belfast City Council, Parks and Amenities Section

City Centre
City Hall left centre; main shopping area top left; main office area bottom left; River Lagan just off right of photo.

While inner city housing renewal is one of the most important markers of the turnaround in the fortunes of Belfast in recent years, the transformation of the City Centre is undoubtedly another. The importance of the City Centre, both functionally and symbolically can hardly be over emphasized. The Belfast Urban Area Plan 2001 claims that a revitalized and thriving City Centre will enhance not only the image of the city, but that of the whole of Northern Ireland. At the same time the centre, with some 56,000 workers is the largest concentration of employment in the region. In addition, in an ethnically fractured city, the centre provides a relatively neutral terrain that is, given its location, reasonably accessible to all sections of the community.

As the 1960s progressed it was beginning to be evident that the City Centre was threatened by two trends ~ the growth in road traffic and the first signs of suburban shopping centre development. Both, of course were related ~ the expanding use of cars was at the root of City Centre congestion, but it was also the raison d'être for the emergence of the shopping centre. Planning policy in the 1960s approached the problem by attempting to limit suburban shopping developments and by proposing a major motorway ring road encircling the City Centre that would, it was hoped divert a significant volume of traffic away from the main shopping streets.

Traffic congestion and suburban shopping centres were nothing unique to Belfast. The third threat ~ urban terrorism ~ was another matter altogether. Here, from 1969 onwards, violence rapidly emerged and in many ways the City Centre was literally at the focus of the action.

The City Centre of the early 1990s is a far cry from that of the early 1970s. Then the bombing campaign of the Provisional I.R.A., which appeared to be a concerted attempt to cripple the city's commercial life, led to the destruction of some 300 retail outlets and resulted in a loss of almost one quarter of the total retail floor-space. Security measures introduced in response to the bombing campaign, together with the campaign itself combined to make shoppers reluctant to patronise centrally located retail establishments. This, in turn, led to a sharp drop in turnover, driving 40 retail establishments out of business in 1971 alone. Reinforcing the decline of the City Centre in the 1970s, and, in some ways, related to it was the development of a series of suburban shopping complexes. At the time the government was desperate for development to take place anywhere in the city and in consequence planners took little action to restrain the suburban retail expansion, even though it was recognized that this would further undermine the City Centre's role. Stephen Brown, writing in 1984 has commented:

Bomb damage in office area

The rate of retail decentralization in Belfast exceeded that in any other British city. It is difficult to avoid the conclusion that recent (1970s) retail trends in Belfast have been more akin to the American pattern of unrestricted suburban growth and city centre decline, than they are to the patterns that prevail elsewhere in the United Kingdom.

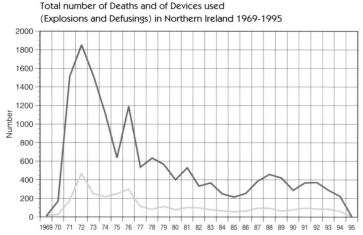

Total number of Deaths and of Devices used
(Explosions and Defusings) in Northern Ireland 1969-1995

Number of Deaths and Explosions in
Belfast Urban Area 1969-1977

Figure 26
Levels of Violence: Northern Ireland 1969-1995;
Belfast 1969-1977

The 1970s was a period of intense violence in Northern Ireland. As Figure 26 shows the worst period was between 1971 and 1976, with 1972 particularly traumatic. Of all the explosions recorded, 41 percent occurred in the Belfast Urban Area. Almost 70 percent of bombings aimed at housing were within the BUA, with targeting of shops, offices, industrial premises and pubs and clubs also being disproportionately concentrated in the City. Though there are no statistics available, it is undoubtedly true that within the BUA the City Centre bore the brunt of attacks on commercial premises.

The 1980s and the early 1990s have witnessed a remarkable recovery in the fortunes of the City Centre. A decrease (and now cessation) of the Provisional I.R.A. bombing campaign, together with a related relaxation in City Centre security arrangements led to renewed confidence among consumers and investors alike. City Centre accessibility was improved

City Centre: the pedestrian heartland

Stephen Brown

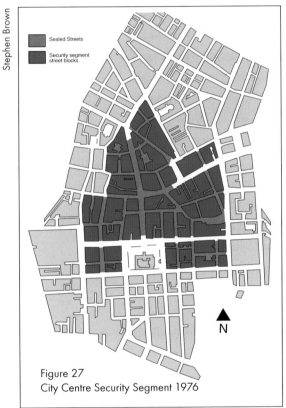

Sealed Streets

Security segment
street blocks

Figure 27
City Centre Security Segment 1976

(new road works, multi-storey car parking provision and some upgrading of public transport), while the environment of the centre was enhanced by extensive pedestrianization, (itself made easier by the security measures taken to exclude car bombers) (Figure 27) and widespread tree planting. A net retail floor-space of 1.3 million square feet in 1967, having declined to 1.1 million by 1975, recovered to 1.3 million again by 1985. This means that much of the evident growth in trade and investment since 1970 has actually been constituted by a recovery to a former position. However since the mid 1980s a further 400,000 square feet of retail space has been added, including a large enclosed shopping complex (Castle Court). By 1994 the retail vacancy rate had dropped to a mere two percent. In sharp contrast, back in 1980, almost 21 percent of retail establishments in the City Centre were unoccupied. The low incidence of vacancy in the mid - 1990s is testimony to the current appeal of Belfast City Centre, and is particularly remarkable considering the amount of additional floor-space added in recent years, both in the central area itself and in competing locations elsewhere in the

City Centre Security: Royal Avenue in the 1970s

Where the gates were: Royal Avenue August 1995

Castle Court: City Centre enclosed shopping and office complex

Regional City. As part of this pattern many national multiples have now become established on prime city centre sites, providing a further indication of commercial confidence and interest. Overall, improvements in the main shopping core have played a major role in the revitalization of the City Centre - a revitalization to be sustained within the guidelines provided by the recently published strategy document *Belfast City Centre: Vision for the Future.*

There has also been a boom in City Centre office construction, particularly on the south side. In the mid 1980s the City Centre had 55 percent of all the office space in Belfast Urban Area. Nonetheless, concern was expressed about the office decentralization that had occurred between 1970 and 1985, a process that threatened to weaken the City Centre. The 2001 Plan stressed that the concentration of office development in the central area would strengthen the heart of the urban economy, while at the same time providing employment easily accessible to all sections of the urban population. Moreover, according to the 2001 Plan, a growing

Crown Copyright / HMSO

Figure 28
City Centre Vision: the commercial framework

City Centre: Donegall Place from City Hall

central business district would underpin and strengthen the public transport services that radiate from the City Centre. This strengthening of the City Centre office component has been aided by the relocation of some government office jobs from sites in the suburban fringe, and by relocation of selected back-office activities from the London area (for instance social welfare claims processing). In consequence of these moves, take-up of new office space in the early 1990s has been dominated by the public sector. Recently, however, as government office needs have been increasingly satisfied, the private sector has far and away become the most likely source of occupants for the newly constructed office accommodation.

City Centre: new office development near Europa Hotel

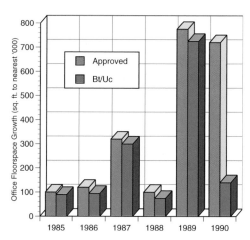

Figure 29
City Centre office floorspace growth 1985-1990
(Bt/Uc = Built or Under construction)

Laganside is adding a new dimension to the City Centre. The west bank of the river is highly accessible to the existing core, and the Laganside proposals clearly see an integration of the existing City Centre with the river-front. On the other hand, some recent reviews of office development in the downtown seem to view the Laganside area not really as part of the City Centre at all, but as a river location for new office construction - *With the planned quality waterfront environment, it seems likely some competition will be offered to the City Centre in the future*, and locations to the south and west of the City Hall, while likely to remain attractive to office occupiers are under challenge from sites such as Clarendon Dock and Laganbank

An important contributor to the revitalization of the City Centre has been the use of the Urban Development Grant (UDG), which was introduced into Northern Ireland in 1982. The low development confidence prevailing in Belfast in the early 1980s led to the UDG being focused on the City Centre and some major arterial routes. Under the standard rate of grant up to 50 percent of construction costs and fees was available to owner occupiers for restructuring purposes and up to 30 percent on speculative development. At one stage the grant was targeted specifically at the decayed north-side of the Centre, while more recently it has been focused on disadvantaged inner city localities. Arguably, the UDG was a key influence in kick-starting the development process in Belfast, forming the platform for an unprecedented period of growth in the retail and office sectors. It is also notable, however, that in the late 1980s many speculative schemes proceeded without recourse to the grant, reflecting the revived property market in Belfast.

City Centre Skyline

Skylines are urban signatures. They are the shorthand of urban identity, and the chance for urban flourish. Cities of all descriptions and periods raise aloft distinctive landmarks, to celebrate faith and power and special achievement. If this be so, what, in particular, is Belfast's signature? Undoubtedly, the dominant building is the City Hall, standing as a green-domed statement of late Victorian civic confidence and pride. It is not particularly high, however, and is at risk from domination by high rise office towers. This has been recognized in the various planning documents of the past quarter of a century. The 1969 Urban Area Plan called for a protection zone round the City Hall whereby no buildings higher than the civic master piece were to be permitted within 320 metres (350 yards). The 2001 plan, similarly, attempts to control high office building by setting a maximum plot ratio of 3 to 1. Belfast's skyline signature, thus, is rather low key, though a few office towers seem to have escaped the official limits, creating an oddly scattered central profile. Perhaps the dominant built elements in the skyline are not set in the City Centre at all. Rather, they make their technological statement over the shipyard building dock.

Some expression of cynicism has been heard with regard to the City Centre revival. In addition, concern has been raised regarding the impact of all the new development on those aspects of Belfast's Victorian heritage judged to be worth preserving. A growing urban conservation movement is in evidence, and a number of Conservation Areas have been designated by government. The objective of these designations is to protect and enhance the essential character of the areas concerned and the important buildings within them, whilst enabling growth and change to occur in appropriate locations, as long as such change is in sympathy with the character and appearance of the existing areas. The first designation covered an area to the south of the City Centre, encompassing the neighbourhood of the Queen's University. Subsequent designations (the Cathedral Conservation Area in 1990 and the Linen Conservation Area in 1992) have been within the City Centre itself. At a time when the city is striving to move away from an extremely traumatic recent past, it is striking and significant that it is also reaching back to a heritage in the built environment, a heritage that provides a reminder of the city's historical underpinnings. For instance, the area covered by the Linen Conservation Area played a very important role in the social and economic development of the linen trade. Here were the premises of flax and yarn merchants, linen merchants and linen conveyors, where arrangements were made for the importing of flax, mainly from Belgium and Russia, and for the exporting of fabrics to many countries of the world.

Belfast City Centre has many roles ~ as symbol of the city itself, as economic engine, and as neutral territory at the heart of ethnic fragmentation. However, despite the fact that it is a shared space for the two major ethnic communities in the city, and probably because of its symbolism, the Centre has suffered greatly from Irish nationalist terrorist attacks. One building in particular has found itself ensnared in competing projects ~ the Grand Opera House, opened in 1895, closed at the height of the violent conflict in 1971, reopened in 1980. Its reopening was generally seen as symbolic of a return to some semblance of normality in the City Centre. Such a perception was also its undoing, since the Provisional I.R.A. have in recent times twice severely damaged the structure with massive car bombs. Nonetheless, in 1995, the Opera House is up and running once again. Thus, Belfast weaves between normality and a penchant for self-destruction.

Belfast Division Planning Office

Belfast Division Planning Office

Cathedral and Linen Conservation Areas

N.I. Tourist Board

Ballet at the Opera House

Down by the River

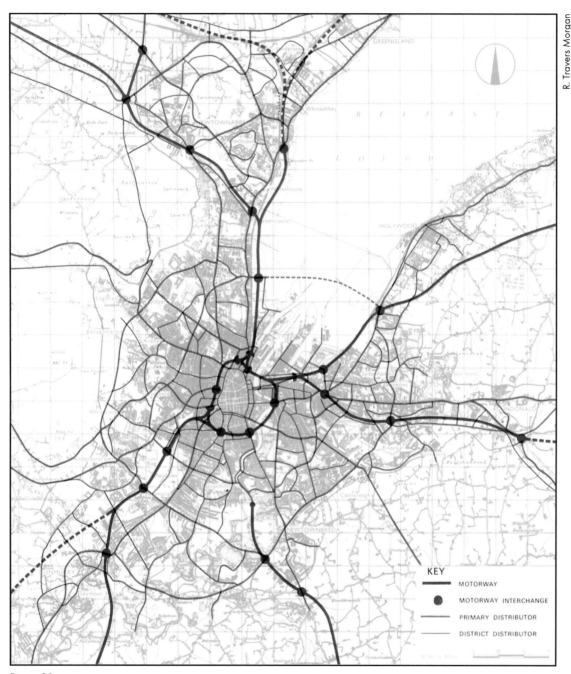

R. Travers Morgan

Figure 30
Road Proposals for 1986 as published in 1969

S ustainable development has been defined as that kind of development that meets the needs of the present without compromising the ability of future generations to meet their own needs. This means that inter-generational equity must be a key feature of sustainability. This is also true for social justice which demands that resources currently available are distributed more evenly amongst populations. Finally, there is the principle of transfrontier responsibility - here the environmental costs of urban activity (waste and pollution) should not be displaced across metropolitan boundaries, while urban resource demands should not lead to overexploitation of other locations.

Transportation

A central concern when considering urban sustainability has been the transportation system. Of course, in parallel with this, it is obvious that the transport and communications networks have been key contributors to the shaping of the city from its earliest days.

If we start with the 1960s we find that transport planning in Belfast emphasized a roads-based approach, the central element of this being an elevated urban motorway encircling the City Centre. A mid-1970s review of the transportation strategy broadened horizons somewhat by offering three possible approaches - a road oriented scheme very similar to the 1960s proposals, an alternative strategy that emphasized buses and a plan dependent upon a balanced use of private vehicles and buses. In none of the strategies was the rail system given an enhanced role. However, the results of the transportation review, following scrutiny by public inquiry, was subsequently modified to include an

R. Travers Morgan

The Low-level Cross-Harbour
bridge as proposed in 1966

improvement in the rail network, this to be achieved by linking the various parts of the system together. This Cross-Harbour Link was to parallel a cross-harbour road bridge that would, in turn, link the motorway system on the west side of the Lagan with the road network in the eastern part of the city.

Lagan Weir with Cross-Harbour rail and road bridges beyond 1995 (compare with the 1966 proposal)

A further review of transportation strategy was published in 1987, now looking to the period 1986-2001. This proposed that transportation in the Belfast Urban Area be provided by a road based system (car, bus, truck) supplemented by the rail network - a conclusion similar to that reached in the mid 1970s. The cross-harbour road and rail bridges were to go ahead, long-stay car parking in the City Centre was to be discouraged, and city centre penetration by the existing rail service was to be expedited by reopening a station on the western edge of the Central Business District (see Figure 28 page 92). Light rail transport solutions were deemed to be inappropriate for Belfast.

A curious feature of transport in Belfast has been the so-called Black Taxi system. This was introduced at the height of the political disturbances in the early 1970s, partly as a replacement for a public bus system that found it increasingly difficult to provide a satisfactory service in certain areas, and partly as a politically motivated gesture against the government. The taxis (mostly cast off London vehicles) operate a kind of jitney system (whereby the taxis work a fixed route system, picking up paying customers when flagged down) along a number of radial routes in the west and north of the city. The 1978 Public Inquiry into the transportation strategy called for the elimination of Black Taxi competition, to be achieved by the enforcement of presently existing law and by the acquisition of new powers. However, in mid-1995 the Black Taxis still operate, much to the financial detriment of the bus system. They provide a popular alternative in their own territory, they create some employment and, not insignificantly, they have been perceived, at least in the past, to have had the backing of paramilitary muscle.

"Black Taxi" City Centre terminal. (Castle Court Car Parking structure beyond)

Transportation strategy in Belfast over the past quarter of a century has evolved from a roads only approach to one that makes some attempt to move away from high car dependency - for reasons environmental, social, economic and functional. And yet, the opening of the cross-harbour road link in early 1995, providing as it undoubtedly does a more co-ordinated and free-flowing network, is really only now putting into place Phase Two of the Urban Motorway as proposed by the traffic consultants as far back as 1966!! Thus, the transport system in Belfast cannot, in its totality, be considered to be particularly environmentally friendly, either in conception or in function. Indeed, transportation policy in Belfast has been curiously indeterminate, not to say contradictory. For

DOE Roads Division

example, City Centre shopper car use has been facilitated by providing over 4000 parking places in multi-storey structures, while the *Vision for the Future* statement for the City Centre calls for a better balance between public transport usage and that of the private car. On a more positive note it is fair to say that pedestrians have been greatly facilitated in the City Centre by the exclusion of most motor vehicles most of the time. Moreover, the bustle of construction activity on transport infrastructure over the past few years has added to the image of the city as one vigorously recovering from the dark days of the early 1970s. A note on the downside - Belfast's accommodation of cycling is well-nigh invisible.

Cross Harbour Rail and Road Bridges with M2 Motorway beyond. The Lagan Weir is immediately upstream with the earlier Queen Elizabeth and Queens' Bridges.

City Centre multi-storey car park

A transport strategy heavily reliant on the use of private cars not only carries a large environmental price tag - it also raises issues of social equity. In a recent survey carried out in the Core City, 48 percent of residents reported that they owned a car. However, this figure conceals a variation between 18 percent in the west inner Core City and 72 percent in the outer eastern suburbs. In such circumstances personal mobility and the way in which the city's geography is evaluated will vary radically from one part of the urban area to another. As transport expert John Whitelegg has written recently:

The car and the lorry are symbolic of the central problem of unsustainability...They represent consumption on a vast scale and this consumption is embedded in societal structures, land use structures and ideological structures...

in such a way as to make change very difficult indeed. And yet, government policy in the mid-1990s seems to be shifting away from the previous roads emphasis. The UK government's new *Planning Policy Guideline on Transport* calls for a less road-dependent system and points the way forward:

Motorway approach to City Centre from North: the M2

By planning land use and transport together in ways which enable people to carry out their everyday activities with less need to travel, local planning authorities can reduce reliance on the private car and make a significant contribution to the environmental goals set out in the Government's Sustainable Development Strategy.

Citybus at Castle Court

If followed in Belfast this should produce a planning policy that gives increasing emphasis to public transport, walking, cycling and a concomitant more compact urban form. However, we can only wait and see.

Urban Metabolism

The metabolism of cities is essentially linear - taking resources from one place and discharging the waste products from their use somewhere else. We can get some indication of the metabolism of the Belfast Urban Area by adapting data from Greater London. The adaptation is achieved by assuming that the Belfast inputs and outputs are about one-twentieth of those of London (the population of the BUA being about one-twentieth that of the UK's capital city).

Belfast Metabolism	
Inputs	**tonnes/year**
Water	50,100,000
Oxygen	2,000,000
Fuel (oil equivalent)	795,000
Food	120,000
Phosphate	3,600
Timber	60,000
Tropical hardwoods	10,000
Paper	110,000
Plastics	105,000
Glass containers	10,500
Plate glass	7,500
Cement	97,000
Bricks, blocks, sand, tarmac	300,000
Metals	60,000
Waste Output	
Inert wastes	410,000
Commercial and industrial wastes	150,000
Total household wastes	121,000
Digested sewage sludge	375,000
CO_2	3,000,000
SO_2	20,000
NO_x	14,000

Adapted from Herbert Girardet "Keeping up with capital growth" Geographical, June 1994

Some of the more blatant manifestations of waste production have, over recent years, been greatly reduced. For instance, visible air pollution is much less severe, due to the introduction of smokeless zones. Solid waste is another matter. In the harbour area, the Dargan Road landfill has reached its capacity limits (which are derived partly from environmental concerns), and the city now has to reach out beyond the Urban Area boundary for alternative landfill sites. In consequence, the transfrontier dimension of urban sustainability is very much in evidence.

Alan Lewis

Smoke over Belfast: Summer 1995 fire at Dargan Road Landfill

One way to contribute to a more environmentally friendly Urban Area is to provide the conditions for a greener city. In 1992, the *Nature in the City* report was issued which presented a nature conservation strategy for the BUA. A **Forest of Belfast** initiative was commenced, which included large-scale street tree planting. This requires great perseverance from the City Parks Department, as "saturday night vandals" seek to carry out their own peculiar deforestation agendas. Important natural habitats within the urban limits are to be protected and, indeed, enhanced. As *Nature in the City* points out, the uniquely compact setting of Belfast, with its surrounding hills and lough shore, provides the Urban Area with a rich assemblage of wildlife habitats. On the other hand, land demand pressures, partly a product of the imposition of limits to urban sprawl, and partly due to the changing composition of households noted earlier in this volume, have led to a significant loss of open space within the city. Thus, in some of the lower density housing areas, the gardens (yards) of many larger houses have been sold off and used for apartment construction or the insertion of additional detached dwellings. This process of densification, while contributing to the maintenance of population numbers in the Core City is, unfortunately, not operating in favour of greening objectives.

Figure 31
Nature in the City map

B.K.S. Surveys Ltd.

Older Inner-Suburban Lower Density Housing: Malone

Sustainable Society?

It is becoming increasingly apparent that urban sustainability has to be defined in cultural and social, as well as ecological terms. Unemployment, alienation, boredom, homelessness and crime are all elements contributing to the unsustainability of cities. As Herbert Girardet claims:

> *Cities are, above all else, places for people, and the day to day quality of people's lives is of paramount concern.*

The dynamics of Belfast over the past thirty years or so, as reviewed in this volume, point to a continuous battle between order and anarchy, between sustainability and unsustainability. Environmental concerns, now emergent, have, in the past, been muted by the clamour of ethnic strife and the deep concerns of economic crisis. Belfast's social sustainability became a big question, but somehow things did not fall apart. It should not be forgotten, however, that Belfast relied, to a significant extent, on the ministrations of a life support machine in the form of massive financial subventions from the UK government and, to a lesser extent, from the European Union. These included, compensation payments for personal injury and property damage, a massive welfare bill, subsidization of housing programmes and employment creation and employment maintenance initiatives - the list is long. In the classic environmental use of the term, Belfast has been far from sustainable.

And yet, as we approach the Millenium in peaceful conditions, hopefully long-lasting, the citizens of Belfast and its surrounding region can look forward with some optimism to a situation where ecology, economy and ethnicity can be harnessed in a productive and sustainable tandem.

A better view of Belfast?

Concluding word

"...tap the cultural diversity of the city as an asset,
rather than manage it as a liability"

(from Paul Sweeney and Frank Gaffikin *Listening to People* 1995)

APPENDIX

The Appendix contains a selection of the data that has been used in compiling the text. It is difficult to obtain data in order to make temporal comparisons as the spatial units employed for data collection by various agencies have changed (Ward boundaries, for instance) and the major spatial units (Core City, Belfast Urban Area) have been redefined in a number of ways over the past 30 years. For the future what is needed is data availability for a fine mesh of spatial units. These units can then be used as "building blocks", enabling the construction of statistical descriptions for a wide and flexible set of larger areas. These basic spatial building blocks should remain immutable over time.

Year	Belfast Core	% Of Total BUA Pop	BUA	% Of Total NI Pop	NI Total Pop
1926	415,000	90.2	460,000	36.6	1,256,561
1937	438,000	89.0	492,000	38.4	1,279,745
1951	444,000	83.5	532,000	38.8	1,370,921
1961	416,000	73.8	564,000	39.6	1,425,042
1971	417,000[2]	69.5	600,000[1]	39.1	1,536,065
1981	314,000[3]	61.9	507,000[1]	33.1	1,532,619
1991	279,000[4]	58.6	476,000[5]	30.3	1,573,282

Table 1. Population for Belfast Core City, Belfast Urban Area and Northern Ireland 1926-1991

Year	Belfast Core	% Of Total BUA Pop	BUA	% Of Total Regional City	Regional City	% Of Total NI Pop	NI Total NI Pop
1971	416,679[2]	69.5	599,718[1]	77	779,125[6]	50.7	1,536,065
1981	314,270[3]	61.9	507,386[1]	69.6	729,005[7]	47.6	1,532,619
1991	279,237[4]	58.7	475,967[5]	65.4	727,391[7]	46.2	1,573,282

Table 2. Population for Belfast Core City, Belfast Urban Area, Belfast Regional City and Northern Ireland 1971-1991

1. Planning Headquarters and NIHE Figure
2. DCA figure: Source Table 4 Summary Tables 1971
3. Table 2 BUA Report 1991 (Revised)
4. Table 2 BUA Report 1991
5. Table 3 BUA Report 1991
6. Table 4 DCA 1971 Census
7. Table 2 Summary Report 1991 Census

	1971	1981	1991
Regional City	779	729	727
Belfast Urban Area	600	507	476
Belfast Core City	417	314	279
Belfast Inner Core City	150	83	64
Belfast Outer Core City	274	231	215
Belfast Urban area suburbs	182	193	197
Outer Regional City	180	222	251

Table 3. Belfast Regional City and Component Parts 1971-1991: Population (000's)

	1971-1981	1981-1991	1971-1991
Regional City	-6	- -	-7
Belfast Urban Area	-15	-6	-21
Belfast Core City	-25	-11	-33
Belfast Inner Core City	-42	-23	-55
Belfast Outer Core City	-16	-7	-22
Belfast Urban area suburbs	+6	+2	+8
Outer Regional City	+23	+13	+39

Table 4. Belfast Regional City and Component Parts 1971-1991: Population Change (%)

	1971	1981	1991
Regional City	231	238	266
Belfast Urban Area	178	167	178
Belfast Core City	125	106	107
Belfast Inner Core City	46	27	28
Belfast Outer Core City	79	79	79
Belfast Urban area suburbs	53	61	71
Outer Regional City	53	71	88

Table 5. Belfast Regional City and Component Parts 1971-1991: Households (000's)

	1971-1981	1981-1991	1971-1991
Regional City	+3	+12	+15
Belfast Urban Area	-6	+7	- -
Belfast Core City	-15	+1	-14
Belfast Inner Core City	-41	+4	-39
Belfast Outer Core City	- -	- -	- -
Belfast Urban area suburbs	+15	+16	+34
Outer Regional City	+34	+24	+66

Table 6. Belfast Regional City and Component Parts 1971-1991: Change in Number of Households (%).

	Roman Catholic	Church of Ireland	Presbyterian	Methodist	Others
1926[1]	95,682	133,100	137,384	25,701	23,284
1937[1]	104,372	140,310	137,939	29,966	25,499
1951[1]	115,029	131,885	134,831	34,504	27,422
1961[1]	114,336	112,296	120,092	33,019	36,113
1971[2]	115,259	95,204	102,975	28,376	24,385
1981	118,600[4]	58,987[3]	59,673[3]	17,473[3]	21,381[3]
1991[5]	108,954	50,242	47,743	14,667	20,113

Table 7. Belfast Core City 1926-1991: Religion

1. Source Vaughan and Fitzpatrick Irish Historical Records.
2. DCA Table 2 Religion Tables 1971 Census.
3. Table 2 Religion Report 1981 Census.
4. Adjusted figure for non response from Table 3 p94 J. Power and P. Compton Economics and Social Review.
5. Table 2 Religion Report 1991 Census.

	Roman Catholic	Church of Ireland	Presbyterian	Methodist	Others	Not Stated	Total Pop
1971[2]	164,920	236,271	189,903	52,833	53,122	72,500	769,549
1981[1]	122,754	190,256	155,112	42,754	65,510	129,633	706,019
1991	181,280	182,435	148,952	42,933	68,432	103,359[3]	727,391

Table 8. Belfast Regional City 1971-1991: Religion

1. Not Adjusted for Non Response.
2. DCA Table 2 Religion Report 1971 Census.
3. None Category and Not Stated Category totals added together.

Table 9. New Housebuilding Starts 1979-1993: Belfast Regional City and Components.

Year		1979	1980	1981	1982	1983	1984	1985	1986
	Private Sector	166	137	205	321	383	497	581	475
Core City	N.I. Housing Executive	454	959	1263	1516	1556	1436	748	1289
	Housing Assocs/others	19	20	166	377	61	207	155	229
Year		**1987**	**1988**	**1989**	**1990**	**1991**	**1992**	**1993**	**Total**
	Private Sector	197	609	476	403	95	488	172	5205
Core City	N.I. Housing Executive	946	1043	588	426	316	309	148	12997
	Housing Assocs/others	203	136	198	456	377	334	129	3067
Year		**1979**	**1980**	**1981**	**1982**	**1983**	**1984**	**1985**	**1986**
	Private Sector	1372	971	1132	1390	2090	2253	2463	2739
S'burbs + Outer Reg. City	N.I. Housing Executive	124	732	476	672	1085	632	682	158
	Housing Assocs/others	165	17	353	109	166	115	62	111
Year		**1987**	**1988**	**1989**	**1990**	**1991**	**1992**	**1993**	**Total**
	Private Sector	3070	2844	2615	2113	2078	2202	2459	31791
S'burbs + Outer Reg. City	N.I. Housing Executive	288	456	124	182	346	180	154	6291
	Housing Assocs/others	81	65	105	102	118	165	195	1929
Year		**1979**	**1980**	**1981**	**1982**	**1983**	**1984**	**1985**	**1986**
	Private Sector	1538	1108	1337	1711	2473	2750	3044	3214
Regional City	N.I. Housing Executive	578	1691	1739	2188	2641	2068	1430	1447
	Housing Assocs/others	184	37	519	486	227	322	217	340
Year		**1987**	**1988**	**1989**	**1990**	**1991**	**1992**	**1993**	**Total**
	Private Sector	3267	3453	3091	2516	2173	2690	2631	36996
Regional City	N.I. Housing Executive	1234	1499	712	608	662	489	302	19288
	Housing Assocs/others	284	201	303	558	495	499	324	4996

Starts are classified as Private Sector, Northern Ireland Housing Executive and Housing Associations plus "others".
Data sources: Regional City - Northern Ireland Housing Executive Belfast Regional Office; Belfast Core City - J. Mc Peake.

Financial Year	Belfast Core City	BUA Suburbs	Rest of Northern Ireland	Total
1971-1972	50	439	1221	1710
1972-1973	803	1202	3584	5589
1973-1974	435	1177	4196	5808
1974-1975	371	691	3950	5012
1975-1976	462	740	3820	5022
1976-1977	744	794	5686	7224
1977-1978	793	370	5561	6724
1978-1979	616	521	3995	5132
1979-1980	780	199	1973	2952
1980-1981	766	265	1670	2701
1981-1982	926	266	1150	2342
1982-1983	1749	547	1332	3628
1983-1984	1489	528	1857	3874
1984-1985	1399	522	1463	3384
1985-1986	1479	406	1275	3160
1986-1987	985	336	901	2222
1987-1988	989	141	675	1805
1988-1989	838	249	566	1653
1989-1990	806	122	649	1577
1990-1991	691	114	519	1324
1991-1992	468	58	435	961
1992-1993	342	167	449	958
1993-1994	257	25	606	888
1994-1995	117	73	640	830

Table 10. Northern Ireland Housing Executive New Dwelling Completions 1971-1995

Area Year	BUA 1961	BUA 1966	BUA 1971	BUA 1975	BUA 1981	BUA 1985	BUA 1991	BUA 1993
1. Manufacturing and Construction	124,200	122,600	88,008	82,635	63,570	55,321	41,500	36,000
2. Services	133,000	144,600	132,723	141,258	151,617	166,275	175,700	179,700
1 + 2.	257,000	267,200	220,731	223,893	215,187	221,596	217,200	215,000

Total Number of Employees in Manufacturing and Construction and in Services

Area Year	BUA 1961	BUA 1966	BUA 1971	BUA 1975	BUA 1981	BUA 1985	BUA 1991	BUA 1993
1. Manufacturing and Construction	48.3	45.9	39.9	36.9	29.5	25.0	19.1	16.7
2. Services	51.7	54.1	60.1	63.1	70.5	75.0	80.9	83.3
1 + 2.	100.0	100.0	100.0	100.0	100.0	100.0	100.0	100.0

Percentage of Employees in Manufacturing and Construction and in Services.

Table 11 Belfast Urban Area 1961-1993: Employees in Manufacturing and Construction and in Services.

Sources of Data: 1961 and 1966: Building Design Partnership; 1971: Northern Ireland Census 1971; 1975-1993:
 Department of Economic Developemnt.

	Resident or Workplace	Total	Males	Females	Male:Female Ratio
1971	Resident in Core City	150662	94144	56518	1 : 0.6
1971	Workplace in Core City	184991	115578	69413	1 : 0.6
	Resident or Workplace	Total	Males	Females	Male:Female Ratio
1981	Resident in Core City	132200	78664	53536	1 : 0.68
1981	Workplace in Core City	151566	88811	62755	1 : 0.71
	Resident or Workplace	Total	Males	Females	Male:Female Ratio
1991	Resident in Core City	118829	67647	51182	1 : 0.76
1991	Workplace in Core City	146917	79919	66998	1 : 0.84

Table 12: Belfast Core City 1971, 1981 and 1991 - Economically Active Persons Resident in Core City and Persons with Workplaces in Core City

(Economically Active Persons are those in employment at the time of the Census, those not currently employed but who are actively seeking work, those not seeking work because of temporary sickness and those who had found work but were to start after census day).

Year	Core City			Suburbs			BUA		
	Males	Females	Total	Males	Females	Total	Males	Females	Total
1987	23241	7657	30898	8718	3958	12676	31959	11615	43574
1988	22042	7014	29056	8107	3669	11776	30149	10683	40832
1989	20252	6250	26502	7342	3306	10648	27594	9556	37150
1990	18931	5350	24281	6878	2806	9684	25809	8156	33965
1991	18727	5088	23815	7039	2772	9811	25766	7860	33626
1992	20080	5330	25410	7591	2761	10352	27671	8091	35762
1993	20359	5475	25834	7868	2712	10580	28227	8187	36414
1994	19263	4835	24098	7492	2411	9903	26755	7246	34001
1995	17153	4364	21517	6692	2143	8835	23845	6507	30352

Table 13. Belfast Urban Area, Belfast Core City and BUA Suburbs 1987-1995: Registered Unemployed in April of Each Year

Source: Department of Economic Development Special Tabulations.

A Belfast Bibliography

There is a vast amount of writing on the subject of Belfast. The works listed below are those that are considered to be immediately relevant to the topics examined in **Shaping a City.** They have been listed under what seems to be the most appropriate section heading as used in this volume. A number of items refer to topics in more than one section, but they are listed only once.

Chapter I Where and When

Bardon, J. (1982). *Belfast: An Illustrated History.* Belfast: Blackstaff.

Barton, B. (1989). *The Blitz: Belfast in the War Years.* Belfast: Blackstaff.

Beckett, J.C. and Glasscock, R.E. (Eds.) (1967). *Belfast: Origin and Growth of an Industrial City.* London: BBC.

Beckett, J.C. et al (1983). *Belfast: The Making of the City.* Belfast: Appletree Press.

Boal, F.W. and Royle, S.A. (1986). Belfast: Boom, Blitz and Bureaucracy. In Gordon, G. (Ed.) *Regional Cities in the UK 1890-1980.* London: Harper and Row. pp. 191-205.

Doherty, P. (Ed.) (1990). *Geographical Perspectives on the Belfast Region.* Geographical Society of Ireland Special Publications No. 5. Newtownabbey: Geographical Society of Ireland.

Goldring, M. (1991). *Belfast: From Loyalty to Rebellion.* London: Lawrence and Wishart.

Hepburn, A. C. and Collins, B. (1981). Industrial Society: The Structure of Belfast, 1901. In Roebuck, P. (Ed) *Plantation to Partition.* Belfast : Blackstaff Press Limited. pp. 210-228.

Johnstone, R. (1990). *Belfast :Portraits of a City.* London: Barrie and Jenkins.

Jones, E. (1952). Belfast: A Survey of the City. In Jones, E. (Ed.) *Belfast in its Regional Setting.* Belfast: British Association for the Advancement of Science. pp. 201-211.

Jones, E. (1960). *A Social Geography of Belfast.* London : Oxford University Press.

Maguire, W. A. (1993). *Belfast.* Keele : Ryburn Publishing.

Moss, M. and Hume, J.R. (1986). *Shipbuilders to the World: 125 years of Harland and Wolff.* Belfast: Blackstaff.

Chapter II Population Since the 1960s

Boal, F. W. (1994). Belfast: a City on Edge. In H. Clout (Ed), *Netherlands Geographical Studies 176: Europe's Cities in the Late Twentieth Century*, Utrecht/Amsterdam: Royal Dutch Geographical Society/ Department of Human Geography, University of Amsterdam. pp. 141-155.

Boal, F.W. (1967). Contemporary Belfast and its Future Development. In Beckett, J.C. and Glasscock, R.E. (Eds.). *Belfast: Origin and Growth of an Industrial City.* London: BBC. pp. 169-182.

Boal, F.W. (1987). The Physical and Social Dimensions of a Regional City. In Buchanan, R.H. and Walker, B.M. (Eds.). *Province, City and People: Belfast and Its Region.* Antrim: Greystone Press. pp. 125-149.

Compton, P. A. (1995). *Demographic Review Northern Ireland 1995.* Northern Ireland Economic Council Research Monograph 1. Belfast : Northern Ireland Economic Development Office.

Compton, P. A. (1990). Demographic Trends in the Belfast Region with Particular Emphasis on The Changing Distribution of the Population. In P. Doherty (Ed.), *Geographical Perspectives on the Belfast Region* . Belfast: Geographical Society of Ireland. pp.15-27.

Compton, P. A. and Power, J. (1986). Estimates of Religious Composition of Northern Ireland Local Government Districts in 1981 and Change in the Geographical Pattern of Religious Composition Between 1971 and 1981. *The Economic and Social Review, 17.* pp. 87-105.

Cormack, R. J., Gallagher, A. M. and Osborne, R. D. (1993). *Fair Enough?* Belfast: Fair Employment Commission for Northern Ireland.

Doherty, P. (1990). Social Contrasts in a Divided City. In Doherty, P. (Ed.) *Geographical Perspectives on the Belfast Region.* Geographical Society of Ireland Special Publications No. 5. Newtownabbey: Geographical Society of Ireland. pp. 28-36.

General Register Office Northern Ireland (1975) *Census of Population 1971: Workplace and Transport to Work Tables.* Belfast: HMSO.

Harrison, R.L. (1981). Population Change and Housing Provision in Belfast. In Compton, P.A. (Ed.) *The Contemporary Population of Northern Ireland and Population Related Issues.* Belfast: Institute of Irish Studies, The Queen's University of Belfast. pp. 40-57.

Hepburn, A. C. H. (1994). Long Division and Ethnic Conflict: the Experience of Belfast. In Dunn, S. (Ed.) *Managing Divided Cities,* Keele: Keele University Press in association with the Fulbright Commission. pp. 88-104.

Murtagh, B. (Ed.) (1993). *Planning and Ethnic Space in Belfast.* Jordanstown: University of Ulster.

Northern Ireland Housing Executive (1986). *Greater Belfast Area Household Survey 1985.* Belfast: Northern Ireland Housing Executive.

Northern Ireland Housing Executive (1994). *Greater Belfast Urban Area Housing Review* [September draft]. Belfast: Northern Ireland Housing Executive.

Northern Ireland Registrar General (1973). *Census of Population 1971: County Report: Belfast County Borough.* Belfast : HMSO.

Northern Ireland Registrar General (1982). *Census of Population 1981:Report for Belfast Local Government District.* Belfast : HMSO.

Northern Ireland Registrar General (1992). *Census of Population 1991: Belfast Urban Area Report.* Belfast : HMSO.

Vaughan, W. E. and Fitzpatrick, A. J. (1978). *Irish Historical Statistics: Population 1821-1971.* Dublin: Royal Irish Academy.

Chapter III

The Planning Experience

Boal, F.W. (1990). Belfast: Hindsight on Foresight - Planning in an Unstable Environment. In Doherty, P. (Ed.) *Geographical Perspectives on the Belfast Region*. Geographical Society of Ireland Special Publications No. 5. Newtownabbey: Geographical Society of Ireland. pp. 4-14.

Building Design Partnership (1969). *Belfast Urban Area Plan Volume 1*. Belfast: Building Design Partnership.

Department of the Environment for Northern Ireland (1977). *Northern Ireland: Regional Physical Development Strategy 1975-95*. Belfast: HMSO.

Department of the Environment for Northern Ireland (1987). *Belfast: Urban Area Plan 2001 Preliminary Proposals.*. Belfast: HMSO.

Department of the Environment for Northern Ireland (1987). *The Belfast Urban Area Plan 1986-2001*. Belfast: HMSO

Department of the Environment for Northern Ireland (1990). *Belfast Urban Area Plan 2001*. Belfast: HMSO.

Gaffikin, F. and Morrissey, M. (1989). Changing Places: Urban Planning for Post-Industrialism in Belfast. *Local Government Policy Making* 16:1 pp. 27-37.

Government of Northern Ireland (1945). *Planning Proposals for the Belfast Area - Interim Report of the Planning Commission*. Belfast: HMSO.

Government of Northern Ireland (1951). *Planning Proposals for the Belfast Area - Second Report of the Planning Commission*. Belfast: HMSO

Government of Northern Ireland, Ministry of Home Affairs (1942). *Preliminary Report on Reconstruction and Planning* [W.R. Davidge]. Belfast: HMSO.

Hendry, J. (1984). The Development of Planning in Northern Ireland. In Bannon, M. and Hendry, J. (Eds.) *Planning in Ireland: An Overview*. Occasional Papers in Planning No. 1. Belfast: Department of Town and Country Planning, The Queen's University of Belfast.

Matthew, R. H. (1964). *Belfast Regional Survey and Plan 1962. A Report Prepared for the Government of Northern Ireland*. Belfast: HMSO.

Murray, M. (1991). *The Politics and Pragmatism of Urban Containment*. Aldershot: Avebury.

Singleton, D. (1981). Planning Implications of Population Trends in Northern Ireland. In Compton, P.A. (Ed.) *The Contemporary Population of Northern Ireland and Population Related Issues*. Belfast: Institute of Irish Studies, The Queen's University of Belfast. pp. 102-114.

Chapter IV

Housing The People

Boal, F.W. (1978). Territoriality on the Shankill-Falls Divide, Belfast: The Perspective from 1976. In Lanegran, D.A. and Palm, R. (Eds.) *An Invitation to Geography* (Second Edition). New York: McGraw-Hill. pp. 58-77.

Boal, F.W. (1981). Residential Segregation and Mixing in a Situation of Ethnic and National Conflict. In Compton, P.A. (Ed.) *The Contemporary Population of Northern Ireland and Population Related Issues.* Belfast: Institute of Irish Studies, The Queen's University of Belfast. pp. 58-84.

Brett, C.E.B. (1986). *Housing a Divided Community.* Dublin: Institute of Public Administration.

Carson, C. (1989). *Belfast Confetti.* Oldcastle, Co. Meath: Gallery Press.

Divis Residents Association (1986). *The Divis Report.: Set Them Free.* Belfast: Divis Residents Association.

Environmental Design Consultants (1991). *Belfast Peacelines Study.* Belfast: Environmental Design Consultants.

Glendinning, M. and Muthesius, S. (1994). *Tower Block: Modern Public Housing in England, Scotland, Wales and Northern Ireland.* New Haven: Yale University Press.

Harbinson, R. (1960). *No Surrender.* London: Faber and Faber.

Hendry, J., Neill, W. J. V., and Mc Conaghy, R. (1986). *Private Sector Housebuilding in Northern Ireland. A Supply Side Investigation,* Occasional Paper No. 13. Belfast: Department of Architecture and Planning, The Queen's University of Belfast

Keane, M.C. (1985). Ethnic Residential Change in Belfast 1969-1977: The Impact of Public Housing Policy in a Plural Society. Unpublished PhD Thesis, The Queen's University of Belfast.

Keane, M.C. (1990). Segregation Processes in Public Sector Housing. In Doherty, P. (Ed.) *Geographical Perspectives on the Belfast Region.* Geographical Society of Ireland Special Publications No. 5. Newtownabbey: Geographical Society of Ireland. pp. 88-108.

Murtagh, B. (1994). *Ethnic Space and the Challenge to Land Use Planning: A Study of Belfast's Peacelines.* Jordanstown: University of Ulster.

Murtagh, B. (1994). Image Making Versus Reality: Ethnic Division and the Planning Challenge of Belfast's Peace Lines. In Neill, W.J.V., Fitzsimons, D. and Murtagh, B. *Imaging the Pariah City.* Aldershot: Avebury. pp. 209-237.

Northern Ireland Housing Executive (1972). *First Annual Report 1971-1972.* Belfast: Northern Ireland Housing Executive.

Northern Ireland Housing Executive (1974). *Northern Ireland Housing Condition Survey 1974 Final Report.* Belfast: Northern Ireland Housing Executive.

Northern Ireland Housing Executive (1978). *Belfast Household Survey Preliminary Report 1978.* Belfast: Northern Ireland Housing Executive.

Northern Ireland Housing Executive (1978). *Coping with Conflict.* Belfast: Northern Ireland Housing Executive.

Northern Ireland Housing Executive (1982). *Belfast Housing Renewal Strategy*. Belfast: Northern Ireland Housing Executive.

Northern Ireland Housing Executive (1984). *The Belfast Experience: Housing Renewal in Northern Ireland*.[D. Singleton] Belfast: Northern Ireland Housing Executive.

Northern Ireland Housing Executive (1991). *Brick by Brick, A Short History of the Northern Ireland Housing Executive 1971-1991*.[I. Maginnis] Belfast: Northern Ireland Housing Executive.

Northern Ireland Housing Executive (1991). *Building A Better Belfast.* [C. Shannon] Belfast: Northern Ireland Housing Executive.

Northern Ireland Housing Executive (1993). *Northern Ireland House Condition Survey 1991*. Belfast: Northern Ireland Housing Executive.

Northern Ireland Housing Executive (1994). *Housing Strategy* 1995 - 1998 Belfast: Northern Ireland Housing Executive.

Quinn, F. (1994). *Interface Images*. Belfast: Belfast Exposed Community Photography Group.

Rolston, B. (1992). *Drawing Support: Murals in the North of Ireland*. Belfast: Beyond the Pale Publications.

Singleton, D. (1982). Poleglass: A Case Study of Division. In Boal, F.W. and Douglas, J.N.H. (Eds.) *Integration and Division: Geographical Perspectives on the Northern Ireland Problem*. London: Academic Press. pp. 178-94.

Singleton, D. (1987). Housing Policy and Trends. In Buchanan, R.H. and Walker, B.M. (Eds.) *Province, City and People: Belfast and Its Region*. Antrim: Greystone Press. pp. 151-168.

Smith, D.J. and Chambers, G. (1989). *Equality and Inequality in Northern Ireland 4: Public Housing*. London: Policy Studies Institute.

Chapter V

In and Out of Work

Belfast City Council (1995). *Economic Development Strategy 1995-2000.* Belfast: Belfast City Council.

Boal, F.W., Doherty, P. and Pringle, D.G. (1974).*The Spatial Distribution of Some Social Problems in the Belfast Urban Area.* Belfast: Community Relations Commission.

Community Training and Research Services (1992). *Poverty Amongst Plenty: Surveys of Taughmonagh and Clarawood Estates.* Belfast: CDPA.

Department of the Environment for Northern Ireland, Town and Country Planning Service (1987). *Belfast Urban Area Plan 2001 - Technical Supplement: Industry and Commerce.* Belfast: Belfast Divisional Planning Office.

Doherty, P. (1981). The Unemployed Population of Belfast. In Compton, P.A. (Ed.) *The Contemporary Population of Northern Ireland and Population Related Issues.* Belfast: Institute of Irish Studies, The Queen's University of Belfast. pp. 115-126.

Doherty, P. (1982). The Geography of Unemployment. In Boal, F. W. and Douglas, J.N.H. (Eds.) *Integration and Division: Geographical Perspectives on the Northern Ireland Problem.* London: Academic Press. pp. 225-47.

Eversley, D. (1989). *Religion and Employment in Northern Ireland*, London: Sage Publications.

Hart, M. (1990). Belfast's Economic Millstone? The Role of the Manufacturing Sector Since 1973. In Doherty, P. (Ed.) *Geographical Perspectives on the Belfast Region.* Geographical Society of Ireland Special Publications No. 5. Newtownabbey: Geographical Society of Ireland. pp. 37-53.

Making Belfast Work (1988). *Making Belfast Work: Belfast Areas for Action.* Belfast: Making Belfast Work.

Making Belfast Work (1995). *Strategy Statement.* Belfast: Making Belfast Work.

McGinn, P. (1989). *The Distribution of Deprivation in the Belfast City Council Area.* Belfast : Belfast Centre for the Unemployed and Community Services Department, Belfast City Council.

Murtagh, B. (1994). Beyond the Hype: Targeting Social Deprivation in Belfast's Public Housing Estates. In Neill W.J.V., Fitzsimons, D.S. and Murtagh, B. *Imaging the Pariah City.* Aldershot: Avebury. pp. 185-209.

Murtagh, B. (1994). *Public Sector Housing and Deprivation in Belfast.* Jordanstown: University of Ulster.

Project Team (1977). *Belfast Areas of Special Social Need, Report by Project Team 1976..* Belfast : HMSO.

Registrar General Northern Ireland (1983). *The Northern Ireland Census 1981: Workplace and Transport to Work Report..* Belfast: HMSO.

Robson, B., Bradford, M.and Deas, I. (1994) *Relative Deprivation in Northern Ireland.* Belfast: Policy Planning and Research Unit.

Rolston, B. and Tomlinson, M. (1988) *Unemployment in West Belfast: The Obair Report.* Belfast: Beyond the Pale Publications.

Shankill Community Council (1983). *The Vital Statistics: Shankill Employment Report.* Belfast: Shankill Community Council.

Sweeney, P. and Gaffikin, F. (1995). *Listening to People: A Report on the Making Belfast Work Consultation Process.* Belfast: Making Belfast Work.

Chapter VI

Special Places

Belfast City Council (1995). *Belfast Waterfront Hall*. Belfast: Belfast City Council.

Belfast Harbour Commissioners (1994). *Annual Report and Accounts 1993*. Belfast: Belfast Harbour Commissioners.

Belfast Harbour Commissioners (1994). *Port of Belfast Handbook and Directory*. Belfast: Belfast Harbour Commissioners.

Berry, J. and McGreal, S. (1993). Public Sector Initiatives in the Regeneration of Belfast. In Berry, J., McGreal, S. and Deddis, B.(Eds.) *Urban Regeneration: Property Investment and Development*. London: Pion. pp. 193-214.

Brown, S. (1984). *Retail Location and Retail Change in Belfast City Centre*. Unpublished PhD Thesis, The Queen's University of Belfast.

Brown, S. (1990). Twenty Years of Change: Retailing in the Belfast Region 1969-1989. In Doherty, P. (Ed.) *Geographical Perspectives on the Belfast Region*. Geographical Society of Ireland Special Publications No. 5. Newtownabbey: Geographical Society of Ireland. pp. 54-67.

Building Design Partnership (1967). *Belfast Urban Area Lagan Valley Country Park*. Belfast: Building Design Partnership.

Building Design Partnership (1967). *City of Belfast Pedestrian Ways for Arthur Square Area*. Belfast: Building Design Partnership.

Building Design Partnership (1969). *Belfast Urban Area Plan : Belfast Central Area*. Belfast: Building Design Partnership.

Department of the Environment for Northern Ireland (1978). *River Lagan: Report of a Working Party*. Belfast: HMSO.

Department of the Environment for Northern Ireland (1990). *Belfast Harbour Local Plan 1990-2005*. Belfast: HMSO.

Department of the Environment for Northern Ireland (1991). *Belfast City Centre Local Plan 2005*. Belfast: HMSO.

Department of the Environment for Northern Ireland (1992). *Cathedral Conservation Area*. Belfast: HMSO.

Department of the Environment for Northern Ireland (1992). *Linen Conservation Area*. Belfast: HMSO.

Department of the Environment for Northern Ireland (1993). *Lagan Valley Regional Park Local Plan 2005*. Belfast : HMSO.

Department of the Environment for Northern Ireland (1994). *Belfast City Centre: Vision for the Future*. Belfast : HMSO.

Fitzsimons, D. S. (1994). Spearheading a New Place Vision: the Laganside Corporation. In Neill W.J.V., Fitzsimons, D.S. and Murtagh, B. *Imaging the Pariah City*. Aldershot: Avebury. pp. 77-112.

Gaffikin, F. and Morrissey, M. (1990). *Northern Ireland: The Thatcher Years*. London: Zed Books.

Green, E.R.R. (1949). *The Lagan Valley 1800-1850*. London: Faber and Faber.

Greer, J.V. and Neill, W.J.V. (1990-91). The Plan as Symbol: A Case Study of Belfast. *Pleanáil* 10. pp. 90-112.

Laganside Corporation (1992). *A Guide to Laganside*. London: EMB PLC.

Laganside Corporation (1993). *Clarendon Dock*. Belfast: Laganside Corporation.

Laganside Corporation (1994). *Laganside Annual Report 1993-1994.* Belfast : Laganside Corporation.

Laganside Corporation (1995). *Gasworks.* Belfast: Laganside Corporation.

Mackey, G. (1994). Urban Regeneration in Belfast. *Proceedings of the Institution of Civil Engineers, Municipal Engineer.* 103. pp. 225-232.

Murray, R. (1982). Political Violence in Northern Ireland 1969-77. In Boal, F. W. and Douglas, J.N.H. (Eds) *Integration and Division: Geographical Perspectives on the Northern Ireland Problem.* London: Academic Press Inc. pp. 309-31.

Neill, W. J. V. (1994). Lipstick on the Gorilla? Conflict Management, Urban Development and Image Making in Belfast. In Neill W.J.V., Fitzsimons, D.S. and Murtagh, B. *Imaging the Pariah City.* Aldershot : Avebury. pp. 50-75.

Patton, M. (1993). *Central Belfast: An Historical Gazetteer.* Belfast: Ulster Architectural Heritage Society.

PPRU Dept. of Finance and Personnel, VLO Dept. of Finance and Personnel, Belfast Divisional Planning Office Department of Environment for Northern Ireland (1987). *Belfast Urban Area Office Study.*

Shepheard, Epstein and Hunter and Building Design Partnership (1987). *Laganside.* Belfast: HMSO.

Sweetnam, R. and Nimmons, C. (1985). *Port of Belfast 1785-1985.* Belfast : Belfast Harbour Commissioners.

Valuation and Lands Agency and Department of Surveying, University of Ulster (1993). *The Belfast Office Market* . Belfast: HMSO.

Valuation and Lands Agency and Department of Surveying, University of Ulster (1994). *The Belfast Office Market:.* Belfast: HMSO.

Valuation and Lands Agency and the School of the Built Environment, University of Ulster (1994). *The Belfast Retail Market* . Belfast: HMSO.

Valuation and Lands Agency and the School of the Built Environment, University of Ulster (1995). *The Belfast Retail Market* . Belfast: HMSO.

Valuation and Lands Office and Department of Surveying, University of Ulster (1992) *The Belfast Office Market* . Belfast: HMSO.

Chapter VII

Sustainable City?

Department of the Environment and Department of Transport (GB) (1994) *Planning Policy Guidance: Transport* [PPG 13]. London: HMSO

Department of the Environment for Northern Ireland (1978). *Belfast Urban Area Plan: Review of Transportation Strategy, Public Enquiry*. Belfast: HMSO

Department of the Environment for Northern Ireland (1987). *A Review of Transportation Strategy for Belfast (1986-2001)*. [Halcrow Fox and Associates with Steer, Davies and Gleave Ltd.]. Belfast: Department of the Environment for Northern Ireland.

Department of the Environment for Northern Ireland (1992). *Nature in the City.* Belfast: Department of the Environment.

Department of the Environment for Northern Ireland (1994). *Belfast Residents Survey 1991.* Belfast: HMSO.

Girardet, H. (1992) *The Gaia Atlas of Cities: New Directions for Sustainable Urban Living.* London: Gaia Books.

Girardet, H. (1994). Keeping Up With Capital Growth. *Geographical* 66: 6. pp. 12-15.

Haughton, G. and Hunter, C. (1994). *Sustainable Cities.* London: Jessica Kingsley.

Moss, M. (1995) The Belfast Debate. *Belfast Telegraph* May 29.

Travers Morgan, R. and Partners, Ministry of Development and Belfast Corporation (1967). *Belfast Urban Motorway.* Belfast: R. Travers Morgan.

Travers Morgan, R. and Partners, Ministry of Development and Belfast Corporation (1969). *Belfast Transportation Plan.* Belfast: R. Travers Morgan.

Whitelegg, G. (1993). *Transport for a Sustainable Future: The Case of Europe.* London: Bellhaven Press.

Working Party Report on the Challenge of the Urban Situation in Ireland Today (1990). *The Challenge of the City.* Belfast: Inter-Church Meeting.